A Beginner's Guide To Juicing

50 Recipes to Detox, Lose Weight, Feel Young, Look Great and Age Gracefully

By

Sharon Daniels

Legal Disclaimers and Notices

Table of Contents

Juicing Lifestyle

With such an increased emphasis on health and nutrition, which comes on the heels of the rising obesity epidemic, many people are researching ways to look and feel good. In fact, there hundreds of different products out there, all claiming to help you lose weight, strengthen your hair and nails, better your complexion, boost your immune system and mental strength.

The truth of the matter is, these miracle weight-loss and beauty programs are just money-making schemes from big corporations. In fact, these products can do more damage to your body than good.

So where do you turn?

There's something out there that's way better than man-made products. Something that actually works. And you're holding this miracle in your hands.

Juicing is an all-natural, all-clean method of losing weight, looking beautiful, becoming mentally stronger, and a way of cleansing your system of toxins. And the best part is that it works, and it's been proven to work by thousands of people – not by paid advertisers, but people like YOU.

Juicing is a natural cure, treatment, and prevention aid for almost any of life's ailments, illnesses, and disorders. It's cheap, convenient, and best of all, its benefits are enormous.

Many of us are always on the go, and we're so caught up with life that we end up eating most of our meals in the car, at work, or while running errands. Usually, we end up eating fast foods, and we not only gain unnecessary weight, but we get almost none of the nutrients we are supposed to take in on a daily basis.

But with juicing, we can fulfill our daily fruits and vegetable requirements, take in vitamins, minerals, and nutrients, and boost our immune systems with amazing health benefits – all without having to sacrifice a ton of time.

For example, let's say you've got a busy day ahead of you. You've got to go to work, drop the kids off at school, pick up groceries, and run about a hundred other errands. You'll be eating all your meals in the car today, it seems. On top of all that, you need to get at least a little nutrition in your diet or your doctor's going to flip.

Luckily, you know exactly what to do.

You know that different fruits and vegetables offer different health benefits, so you concoct a juice that fits your individual needs. You combine an apple for memory and heart health, a pear to reduce risk of cancer, a plum for healthy aging, 3 broccoli florets for strong bones, teeth, and vision, and finally a handful of baby carrots for a healthy immune system. You simply run these fruits and veggies through the juicer, and in the course of ten minutes, you've prepared a juice full of amazing health benefits, nutrients, and vitamins. Plus, you save the time of having to wait in drive-thru lines for junk food – instead, you've got an on-demand juice that cleanses the system and leaves you feeling better than ever.

There are so many amazing benefits to juicing, some of which you will learn more about as you read ahead. But in case you've read this far and you're still not convinced, here is a list of unbeatable reasons to convert to a juicing lifestyle.

Top 10 Reasons to Begin a Juicing Lifestyle

- Juicing helps you to absorb more nutrients. Most people, due to a lifetime of unhealthy food choices, have weakened digestive systems. So many nutrients will pass out of the body as waste instead of being absorbed. Juicing will help your body revamp its digestive system so that more nutrients will be absorbed than wasted. This is probably the MOST important reason to begin a juicing lifestyle – it will greatly improve your health and the way you feel day to day.

- If you're lacking in energy – juicing is your answer! An 8 oz. glass of juice is like an injection of pure energy right into your blood stream. You will gain amazing amounts of natural energy without having to go through feeling jittery and sugar crashes.

- The different fruits and vegetable combinations and possibilities are endless! This is one lifestyle that will never become boring and predictable. There are hundreds among hundreds of different types of fruits and veggies and you will have a blast experimenting with different juicing combinations. The health benefit? While you are having fun testing different produce, your body will be introduced to a variety of different fruits and veggies and all of their health benefits.

- There are many more health benefits to eating raw fruits and vegetables than eating cooked or processed produce. When you consume raw fruits and veggies, you are guaranteeing your body the maximum amount of nutrients those fruits and vegetables can offer. Once produce becomes cooked or processed the nutrients begin to dissipate little by little, so juicing provides you with a delicious way to provide your body with the greatest amount of nutrients that raw fruits and veggies have to offer.

- Juicing is a natural cure, treatment, and prevention aid for almost any of life's ailments, illnesses, and disorders. You are able to fill your body with healing and nourishing juices instead of harmful and toxic medications that cause risky side effects.

- You have TOTAL CONTROL over what is going in to your body. You know each ingredient and can build your juicing regimen to meet your own individual needs and desires. Plus, I want to make it clear that there are absolutely zero limits to what you can do. YOUR taste buds are in charge! If you want to throw in some almonds or coconut or yogurt just to see how they taste with a particular fruit or vegetable – then go ahead! If you want to sweeten up a veggie juice with a slice or two of a peach or a pinch of splenda – then go ahead! If you want to throw in a sprinkle of cinnamon or nutmeg, a splash of vanilla, or a drop of lemon – then go ahead!

- You never have to wonder or worry about harmful or toxic chemicals, additives, or preservatives. You KNOW the ingredients so you KNOW what is going in to your body and THAT is valuable to living a healthy lifestyle.

- Juicing can also help you meet daily calcium and protein requirements. One 8 oz. glass of carrot juice offers a protein equivalent of one large egg or a 3 oz. of cooked chicken!

- Juicing can fit with modern America's need of a "fast food" lifestyle. In the hustle and bustle of our busy lives, it can be so much faster and easier to pull through a McDonald's drive-thru than to prepare healthy meals. Juicing can turn this notion upside-down. In the amount of time it takes to pull through a McDonald's drive-thru and order a combo meal you could have a delicious and nutritious juice that meets all of your individual recommended nutrition requirements!

- One of the most important factors as to why you should begin a juicing regimen is because you will be doing something that is 100% for you, for your health. You will be offering you mind and body an amazing gift. Your mind and body work so incredibly hard for you around-the-clock, so this could be a remarkable way to give back. In providing your mind and body with the nutrients they crave, you in turn will be stronger, feel healthier, and look absolutely stunning.

In this book, we'll be running you through the basics, the guidelines, and the golden tips and tricks of juicing. You'll be introduced to fifty delicious recipes that are as rewarding for your health as they are for your taste buds.

This book will also breeze you through the different categories of juicing:

- Juicing for Cleansing and Detoxification
- Juicing for Weight Loss/Weight
- Juicing for Mind
- Juicing for Healthy Aging and Beauty

Now you've seen some of the many ways people use juicing to completely change their lives. Why not join the party? Throughout the rest of this book, you'll be able to browse through recipes for all of the above purposes. Hopefully, you'll be able to add your own twist to these juices as well.

Happy Juicing!

Square One: Finding the Right Juicer

We'll start by identifying the differences between a blender and a juicer. While a blender is handy for quick and easy liquefying, it does not separate the pulp from the juice – which has a big impact on the way the juice will taste. A juicer automatically separates the pulp from the juice, which is a lot easier than straining by hand.

(Why should you care about the pulp, you ask? Many people use the pulp in a variety of creative ways. Some spread it on their gardens as fertilizers, while others use it in other recipes. I know several people who get a kick out of freezing their pulp into popsicles as healthy – and tasty – treats.)

The type of recipe also depends on whether you want a juicer or blender. For example, the thicker smoothie-type drinks will most likely require a blender. On the other hand, thinner, lighter juices are best made in a juicer.

Of course, there are the more daring drinks that require use of both blender and juicer. Many people prefer to first run the fruits and/or veggies through a juicer, and then transfer the juice to a blender so it can be combined with other ingredients (i.e. herbs, powders, nuts and seeds, yogurt, milk, ice, and so on).

It's important to choose the juicer that is right for you. Depending how often you juice, what ingredients you use, and your juice preferences, you'll need a juicer that'll match all your requirements.

All the juicers differ greatly from one another, though at first glance, it may not seem like it. So, what factors do you consider?

Number one is price – juicers can range in price from under $70 to over $700 and everything in between. I myself have experimented with many juicers from the least expensive to the most expensive, and I have found that the best juicers usually fall within the $150 - $350 range.

Now that you've narrowed your options down a bit, let's take a look at some of the must-have features for any juicer.

Finding the Perfect Juicer

Adequate Horsepower: Stay clear of juicers with low horsepower. If they are weak they can be easily destroyed by as little as one puny carrot. I recommend a horsepower of at least .5.

Ability to juice all type of fruits/vegetables: This is very important as you don't want to limit your options. Part of the appeal about juicing is all of the possibilities of combinations – so be sure to get a juicer that will allow you to juice any fruit/veggie you like.

Large Feed Tube: The larger the feeding tube, the easier it is to juice. Try to find a juicer with the largest tube possible to keep you from having to cut your produce into teeny-tiny pieces for it to be able to pass through the feed tube.

A Pulp Receptacle: This saves you the hassle of having to scoop all of the pulp out of the juicer on your own. These type of juicers will collect the pulp from produce in a little receptacle, when the receptacle is full all you have to do is pull out the tray/container, trash or set aside the pulp, and then slide the receptacle back in to the juicer. It's as easy as 1, 2, and 3. This option is definitely one of my personal favorite juicing machine features.

Easy to Clean/Easy to Use: Obviously, this is a big one as you don't want a juicer that takes 10 minutes to juice but an hour to clean. Neither do you want one with hundreds of intricate parts that you need to assemble and reassemble every time you use and clean the juicer. You also don't want a juicer that is as complicated as flying an airplane. The easier the machine is to use, the higher the chances of you sticking to your new juicing lifestyle.

Back to the Basics: Fruits and Veggies

Once you have found the ideal juicer for you, it's time to educate yourself on the basics of juicing. It's a good idea to take a refresher course on fruits and vegetables and the benefits that are derived from different nutrients. Learn about the different produce for different seasons, and learn how to pick out produce at the fruit stand. A simple internet search should help you with that.

Here's something I think is really amazing: for every disease or ailment you name, there is a certain fruit or veggie out there that can help cure it. But you've got to be picky about the ingredients you use – aisles after aisles of produce are loaded with pesticides and other nasty hormones.

Below, I'll give you a rundown of the Dirty Dozen, which are fruits and vegetable that typically contain the highest amount of pesticides. (These are fruits and veggies that should always be purchased organic.) Also listed are the Clean 15, which are different types of produce which usually carry the least amount of pesticides and are highly recommended for juicing. I'll also break down the golden rules of juicing for you.

Remember to take the learning process slow; take as much time as you need.

Let's begin with a sample of some of the benefits that different fruits and vegetables offer. The easiest way that I have found in teaching new juicers about the vitamins, nutrients, and minerals in certain fruits and veggies is by breaking down the colors of produce.

Colors have a lot more to do with juicing than you think, so pay attention.

Colors = Benefits

Red: Red fruits/veggies are full of antioxidants and a special nutrient called lycopene, which together offer many special health advantages. For example, they promote heart health, reduced risk of cancer, urinary tract heath, memory health, and help treat hundreds of ailments such as arthritis and menopause. Some of the many examples or red produce include:

- Apples
- Cranberries
- Strawberries
- Watermelon
- Beets
- Red Peppers
- Tomatoes
- Red Kidney Beans

Green: Green fruits and veggies include nutrients such as lutein and folate, which aid in lowering cholesterol, speeding metabolic rate, healthy vision, strong bones and teeth, reduces cancer risk, and helps in the treatment and prevention of many ailments and illnesses such as hair loss, fibromyalgia, Alzheimer's disease, and Chronic Fatigue Syndrome. Some examples of green produce include:

- Green Apples
- Kiwi Fruit
- Avocados
- Broccoli
- Green Beans
- Sweet Peas
- Asparagus
- Green Edamame

Yellow/Orange: Produce that is orange or yellow in color carries nutrients such as Vitamin A, Vitamin C, and Folate. Some of the benefits of consuming these fruits and veggies include helping one in maintaining a strong immune system, heart health, healthy eyes and vision, and improving one's memory and overall mental function. Yellow and orange produce has also been known to aid in the treatment and prevention of many illnesses/ailments, including poor circulation, blood clots, ulcers, and motion sickness. Some of the many examples of yellow and orange produce include:

- Apricots
- Lemons
- Cantaloupe
- Oranges
- Carrots
- Pumpkin
- Sweet Potatoes
- Yellow Lentils

White/Brown/Tan: Produce that is brown, tan, or white in color is usually rich in nutrients such as potassium and allicin. These nutrients have been associated with heart health, maintaining healthy cholesterol levels, reducing the risk of certain cancers, and lowering blood pressure. Some of the many ailments that brown/tan/white produce helps treat include stress, menstrual cramps, and aches and pains. Below are some of those wonderful brown, tan, and white fruits and veggies:

- Coconut
- Dates
- Brown Pears
- Cauliflower
- Kohlrabi
- White Onions
- Mushrooms
- Lima Beans

- Brown Lentils

-

Purple/Blue/Black: Blue, purple, and black produce are very rich in antioxidants which can assist in weight loss and metabolism, heart health, healthy aging, urinary tract health, and much more. Some of the common ailments that Blue, Purple, and Black fruits/veggies help treat are the sinister cataracts, gout, and varicose veins. There are many of the said produce options available, some of the few include:

- Blueberries
- Plums
- Purple Grapes
- Black Olives
- Eggplant
- Purple Asparagus
- Purple Cabbage
- Black Beans
- Black Soybeans
- Blackberries

By using the colors of produce as a guide, you've given yourself a great head start.

The Dirty Dozen – Produce High in Pesticide Residue

Some fruits and veggies carry higher amounts of pesticide residue than others, As a general rule of thumb, experts have compiled a list of 12 fruits and vegetables that should ALWAYS be purchased organic. Buying organic produce lessens your intake of pesticides by over 80%, which is phenomenal. However, organic produce can be quite pricey, so experts gathered a list of the 12 fruits and vegetables that are at risk for carrying the highest amount of pesticides. These fruits and veggies are commonly referred to as "The Dirty Dozen":

- Apple
- Bell Pepper
- Blueberries (domestic)
- Celery
- Cherries
- Grapes (imported)
- Lettuce
- Nectarine
- Peach
- Potato
- Spinach, Kale, and Collard Greens
- Strawberries

The Clean 15 – Produce Low in Pesticide Residue

The following is a list of 15 fruits and vegetables that are known to typically have the lowest pesticide content. These are fruits and veggies that are fine to purchase as non-organic. These 15 fruits and vegetables are known as "The Clean 15":

- Asparagus
- Avocado
- Broccoli
- Cabbage
- Eggplant
- Kiwi
- Mango
- Onion
- Papaya
- Pineapple
- Sweet Corn

- Sweet Peas
- Sweet Potato
- Tomato
- Watermelon

Fruits and Veggies: From Prep to Juicer

Once you have purchased your produce, it is time to prepare it for juicing. Here are a few basic guidelines and to-dos for preparation:

Rinse/wash ALL produce before juicing to remove any pesticide build-up. There are produce washing fluids available at most grocery and health food stores, but rinsing vigorously with cool water is just as useful.

Be sure to cut away and discard any bruised or damages areas on produce.

Always remove the peels of grapefruits, oranges, and tangerines before juicing. The skins of these fruits are very bitter and can wreak havoc on one's digestive system. Lemon/lime peels can be juiced ONLY if they are organic, but they can add an unappealing flavor to your juice. It's important to leave as much of the white, stringy-filmy part of these citrus fruits as possible as it is loaded with bioflavonoids and Vitamin C. The peels of papayas and mangoes MUST be peeled away and discarded – they contain an irritant which can be harmful in continuous consumption. A good rule-of-thumb to follow is to remove the peels and skins of all sprayed produce unless it is organic.

Remove any hard seeds, pits, and stones from produce such as peaches, plums, cherries, etc. Softer seeds, such as those from watermelon, cucumbers, grapes, and oranges, can be juiced without concern. Apple seeds can be juiced for adults, but should be avoided in juices for children as the seeds contain chemicals that can be harmful to kids.

Stems and leaves of most produce CAN and SHOULD be juiced. There are many nutrients available in the leaves and stems of many different veggies and fruits. However, thicker grape stems can dull juicer blades, so be careful. Also, the greens from rhubarb and carrots should always be removed and discarded as they contain toxic substances.

Cut produce in chunks/sections that will easily fit through your juicer's feeding tube. Trying to cram too large of produce down the feeding tube will eventually destroy your juicer. Remember, the larger the feed tube, the bigger the bits of produce that can be fed into the juicer.

Remember that some produce do not juice as well as others. A good guideline to follow is the more water a fruit or veggie contains, the easier it is to juice, and vice versa. Some examples of produce that do not juice as well include avocados, bananas, and coconut. It is important when processing these types of produce to first run the easy-to-juice produce, and then transfer the juice into a blender. Then blend the hard-to-juice produce with the extracted juices.

The most important guideline to follow is to drink your juice as soon as possible after the juicing process is completed in order to benefit the most from the vitamins and minerals. Light, heat, and air can kill nutrients very quickly, so if you can't drink up right away, it's best to store your juice in an airtight container in the fridge. Remember: the longer a juice sits, the more oxidized it becomes, the more nutrients are lost. So drink up!

The Juicing Solution

There you have it - some of the basic how-tos, guidelines, and rules-of-thumb to use in beginning a healthy and fulfilling juicing lifestyle. Perhaps the MOST important factor of juicing was not touched upon as much as it should have been. It is imperative for juicers, particularly new juicers, to remember, above all else, to HAVE FUN! It doesn't matter how many fruits and vegetables are sacrificed during the learning process, or how filthy the kitchen becomes, or how filthy you become, or how disgusting the first 37 juice concoctions taste. What matters is that you remember to relax. Remind yourself when you become frustrated or impatient during the learning curve that you are doing something for yourself that will help your mind and body benefit in so many remarkable ways.

Following is a run-down of some of the benefits that juicing offers. Again, most people who begin juicing do so for a particular reason, which usually falls in one or more of the following categories:

Juicing for Cleansing and Detoxification – This is a big category, as most people associate juicing with cleansing and detox. Juicing is one of the safest and healthiest ways to quickly wash out harmful chemicals and replenish helpful bacteria in your digestive system. Whether you are interested in a full body cleanse/detox, an intestinal cleanse, a liver or kidney cleanse, or whatever else, juicing will provide you with a simple, thorough, and safe manner of doing so. Don't forget, though, it's important to remember before beginning any detox or cleansing program to consult your primary physician.

Juicing for Weight Loss/Weight Gain - This is another big category. Though most people turn to juicing for weight loss, many also use juicing as a way to gain weight and bulk up muscle.

Juicing for Mind and Body – This includes juicing for improved mental function, memory recall, focus and concentration, reduced stress, and anxiety. It also involves Remedy Juicing, which includes juicing to prevent, treat, alleviate pain or suffering, or heal illnesses, ailments, and disorders involving anything from a toothache to cancer.

Juicing for Healthy Aging and Beauty - Wrinkles, age spots, acne, uneven skin tone, varicose veins, cellulite, stretch marks, eczema, hair thinning, and hair loss – these are just a few of the reasons people juice for healthy aging and beauty. People in this category juice for soft, smooth, moisturized, even-toned, glowing, and radiant skin. They also want to gain bright eyes, a beautiful smile, and strong, healthy hair and nails. They also juice to assist in a healthy and graceful aging process.

Now you've seen some of the many ways people use juicing to completely change their lives. Why not join the party? Throughout the rest of this book, you'll be able to browse through recipes for all of the above purposes. Hopefully, you'll be able to add your own twist to these juices as well.

Juicing for Cleansing & Detoxification

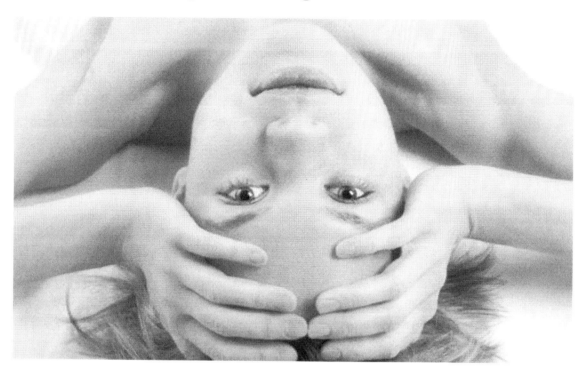

More and more people are turning to juicing for cleansing and detoxing. Certain produce is excellent at ridding your bodies of harmful chemicals and substances. Just as your house needs a deep cleaning every so often, so does your body. There are several different types of detoxing regimens and cleansings; it's just a matter of finding the one that is right for you and ideal for your individual needs.

Detox and cleansing program can include ones that cleanse the entire body as well as ones that are meant for only specific areas of the body. Some of these area-specific cleanses include:

- Liver Cleanses
- Gallbladder Cleanses
- Intestinal Cleanses
- Kidney Cleanses

The most popular types of detoxing involve full-body cleansings. It is easy to come up with your own cleansing regimen –it's all about following the basics of detox and knowing the right types of produce to use in juicing cleanses. A good rule of thumb in juice detoxification is to stick with as many vegetables as possible, because during detox, it is important to steer clear of as much sugar as possible. It's fine to use fruits if you really want to; just make sure the vegetable to fruit ratio is somewhere around 3:1. Some of the most popular types of produce used in detox and cleansing include:

- Green Bell Peppers
- Carrots
- Apples
- Grapefruit (Be sure to ask a doctor about consumption if you're on prescription medications; grapefruit can interact with certain medications and adverse reactions.)
- Lemons/Limes
- Beets
- Wheatgrass
- Sprouts of any kind, including Alfalfa,
- Cabbage
- Parsley (Careful, high consumption of parsley can be toxic, it's recommended intake is no more than ½ cup per day)
- Celery

Creating juices where any of the above ingredients count for a bulk of the juice, will help you in ridding your body of toxins.

The following produce also helps in detox and cleansing diets. They can act as a diuretic which is important in expelling toxins from the body. These include:

- Kiwi Fruit
- Watermelon
- Cantaloupe (with seeds)
- Lemon
- Asparagus

Creating a juicing regimen using the above ingredients will certainly result in successful detoxing and cleansing programs.

Safety First

Remember, as with any cleansing/detox programs, certain precautions and safety measures need to be taken. The most important is to speak with your doctor before beginning any detox or cleansing program. Make sure that you are healthy enough to detox and that you are not at high risk for complications or adverse reactions during the cleansing.

Symptoms of a Juicing Cleanse/Detox

As with any detox program, you are highly likely to experience symptoms and side effects, some of which can be rather unpleasant. The following are some of the common symptoms that you may notice during your juicing cleanse. Remember, if any of the following are too much to bear, discontinue your cleansing program immediately and contact your primary physician at once. In case of an emergency, call 911 and seek help right away.

- Headaches
- Fatigue
- Nausea
- Increased Urination
- Increased Energy
- Moodiness
- Sore Muscles
- Insomnia
- Weakness
- Anxiety/Restlessness
- Diarrhea
- Sore Throat
- Chills/Fever
- Intense Thirst
- Lack of Appetite
- Weight loss
- Dizziness

Remember, if you do experience these side effects, that they are common. As your body makes its way through the cleansing process, these side effects will begin to subside. However, only you know what is normal and what isn't for you – so listen to your body; it will tell you if something is more than just a common side effect from your body ridding itself of toxins.

Juicing Recipes for Cleansing/Detox

Look at some of the common recipes for juicing cleanses. They are very useful in getting started. Experiment – one of the great things about juicing is that there is an unlimited number of fruits/vegetables combinations that can be used in juicing. It's one of the reasons juicing is steadily becoming increasingly popular – the choices are endless, which keeps you from becoming tired or bored with juicing regimens. Some samples of different Cleansing and Detoxification Juice Recipes are as follows.

The Green Cleanse

This juice will help cleanse and support your liver and gallbladder by flushing them with the vitamins, nutrients, and minerals they have been lacking in. The juice helps aid the secretion of bile that your gallbladder and liver need to function properly, as well helping rid your gallbladder of the stones and grit that bile can create. As long as the following main ingredients are used, other ingredients can be added for taste or to meet particular individual needs. For example, someone with a weaker liver may add wedges of apple for additional liver support.

Juice prep to finish: 5 minutes

Difficulty: Easy

Yield: (1) 8 oz. glass

Ingredients:
- 1 handful of parsley, washed
- 4 medium carrots, greens removed, washed, ends trimmed
- 1 small beet root, with some leaves remaining (can also use beet root extract available for purchase at any health food store)
- 1 curled endive leaf
- 2 celery stalks with greens, washed and ends trimmed
- ½ lemon, peeled

Instructions:
1. Process washed parsley into juicer
2. Feed carrots, beet root with leaves, endive leaf, celery stalks with greens, and peeled lemon through juicer.
3. Pour juice into glass, over ice if desired, and stir with spoon to make sure juice is well blended.
4. Drink immediately to benefit from all the nutrients.
5. Any remaining juice can be refrigerated for up 48 hours, in a airtight, opaque container as to not be exposed to light, heat, or air due to risk of oxidation and loss of nutrients.

Nutritional info:
- Calories: 157
- Total Fat: 3.2g
- Total Carbohydrates: 21.8g
- Dietary Fiber: 3.8g
- Sugars: 11.8g
- Protein: 2.3g
- Sodium: 2mg

The Smooth Smoothie-Juice

This is a deliciously-nutrient-rich smoothie juice that will blast your kidneys free of toxins and waste. Some of the benefits include removal of wastes and urine excretion, regulating your pH balance, maintaining the balance and regulation of fluids and electrolytes as well as your blood pressure.

This is a favorite recipe of many juicers. The ingredients in this juice will help to replenish and support kidney function and urinary health. This juice will also help expel wastes and reduce the toxin build-up in your kidneys. If you have kidney disease, please consult with your doctor about kidney cleansing before beginning to cleanse.

Note: *the recipe calls for an optional Green Super food Powder of choice. This type of powder can be purchased at any whole foods market or health food store. This juice can be created by using a juicer and blender or only a blender. For the recipe below, I used both.*

Juice prep to finish: 10 minutes

Difficulty: Easy

Yield: (1) 8 oz. glass

Ingredients:
- 1/2 cucumber, peeled, and cut into chunks
- 1 cup raw spinach
- Juice of 1 lime
- 1/4 avocado – peeled and seeded
- 1 tablespoon green Super food powder of choice (available anytime at any health food store or whole foods market) (optional)
- 1 tablespoon coconut milk
- 1 tablespoons ground almonds (optional)
- Ice, blended (optional)

Instructions:
1. Process cucumber chunks, raw spinach, and lime juice in juicer.
2. Pour juice into blender. Add cut avocado, coconut milk, green superfood powder, and ice (if blending).
3. Pour blended smoothie into cup and top with ground almonds (optional)
4. Enjoy immediately.

Nutritional info:
- Calories: 142
- Total Fat: 9.05g

- Total Carbohydrates: 12.6g
- Dietary Fiber: 4.4g
- Sugars: 2.96g
- Protein: 2.6g
- Sodium: 34mg

A-Get Up-and-Go-Go

This is a great juice blend for the 3rd or 4th day of your cleanse when those side effects are hitting you hard and you are finding it difficult to muster up the energy to just get out of bed in the morning. This juice will help to refresh and energize you – so many juicers have told me that this is the juice that helped them to get over the midweek detox-slump that every detox juicer despises. So c'mon – get up and Go-Go!

Juice prep to finish: 10 minutes

Difficulty: Easy

Yield: (1) 8 oz. glass

Ingredients:
- 3 – 4 carrots, washed, greens removed, and ends trimmed
- 1 cucumber, peeled
- ½ beetroot – stem and leaves attached, washed
- ½ lemon, peeled
- 1-inch piece gingerroot, scrubbed, (peeled, if needed)
- Ice (optional)

Instructions:
1. Cut carrots, cucumber, and beetroot in small enough chunks to fit in your juicer's feed tube, then process.
2. Process lemon and gingerroot into juicer.
3. After juicing all ingredients, pour into a tall glass, over ice if desired, and stir with spoon to ensure juice is well blended. Drink juice as soon as possible to benefit from full amount of nutrients.

Nutritional info:
- Calories: 142
- Total Fat: 2.7g
- Total Carbohydrates: 17.9g
- Dietary Fiber: 2.9g
- Sugars: 8.5g
- Protein: 0.9g
- Sodium: .13 mg

Total Body Kick

This is a wonderful way to a full body detox. Even if you are not in the process of a multi-day body detox/cleanse, you should still consume this juice at least once per week. Consider it weekly maintenance for your body. You can add other ingredients to this juice if you would like to make it more your own. Or you can add a great booster like alfalfa sprouts – either way, this juice should be one you make often.

Juice prep to finish: 10 minutes

Difficulty: Easy

Yield: (1) 8 oz. glass

Ingredients:
- 1 tomato, washed
- 1 medium asparagus spear, washed
- 1 cucumber, washed and peeled
- ½ lemon, peeled
- Ice, optional

Instructions:
1. Process tomato, asparagus, cucumber, and lemon into juicer.
2. Pour into tall glass, over ice if desired, and stir with spoon to ensure juice is well blended.
3. Drink juice as soon as possible to benefit from full amount of nutrients.

Nutritional info:
- Calories: 51.5
- Total Fat: 0.78g
- Total Carbohydrates: 11.2g
- Dietary Fiber: 3.6g
- Sugars: 6.2g
- Protein: 2.6g
- Sodium: 10mg

Spotless Liver

This juice is designed especially to help cleanse, support, and help improve liver function. Drinking this juice helps in expelling any toxins from your liver and helps to replenish and rejuvenate your liver.

Juice prep to finish: 5-10 minutes

Difficulty: Easy

Yield: (1) 8 oz. glass

Ingredients:
- 1 handful of dandelion (greens or tincture available year-round at any health food store)
- 3 to 4 carrots, washed and peeled, greens removed and ends trimmed
- ½ cucumber, peeled
- ½ lemon, peeled

Instructions:
1. Cut carrots and cucumbers in chunks and process through juicer
2. Add dandelion green or tincture to juicer
3. Add lemon to juicer
4. After juicing, pour juice into a tall glass, over ice if desired, and stir with spoon to ensure juice is well blended.
5. Enjoy as soon as possible in order to benefit from full amount of nutrients

Nutritional info:
- Calories: 132
- Total Fat: 46g
- Total Carbohydrates: 30.5g
- Dietary Fiber:: 9.1g
- Sugars: 15.1g
- Protein: 3.2g
- Sodium: 172mg

The Sparkling Clean Bean

A great full body cleanse recipe that will leave you feeling refreshed and revitalized. A hearty mix of great cleansing veggies is a sure fire way to kick of any full body detox. This is a juice that is ideal at any stage of your cleansing program. This is also a great recipe to use to target your pancreas. Note: This is a strong-tasting drink so I recommend using a bit of cold water to dilute and pouring the juice over ice cubes. The colder the juice is the better it tastes.

Juice prep to finish: 15 minutes

Difficulty: Easy

Yield: (1) 8 oz. glass

Ingredients:
- 2 romaine lettuce leaves, washed
- ½ cucumber, peeled
- 1 large vine-ripened tomato, washed
- 8 to 10 string beans, washed and any stems removed
- 2 Brussels sprouts, washed
- ½ lemon, peeled
- Water, optional
- Ice, optional

Instructions:
1. Bunch up romaine lettuce leaves and fit them into your juicers feeding tube,
2. Using the cucumber to help push the lettuce leaves through, juicing both the romaine and cucumber.
3. Process string beans, and Brussels sprouts into juicer.
4. Process peeled lemon through juicer.
5. Lastly, juice tomato.
6. Pour into tall glass, over ice if desired, and stir with spoon to ensure juice is well blended. Use water to dilute if too strong.
7. Drink juice as soon as possible to benefit from full amount of nutrients.

Nutritional info:
- Calories: 86
- Total Fat: 1.2g
- Total Carbohydrates: 14.2g
- Dietary Fiber: 5.8g
- Sugars: 9.2g
- Protein: 3.7g
- Sodium: 17mg

The Orange and Green Cleanse

Great detox juice that also tastes good! The oranges place a nice spin on the juice and are great for giving the body a big jolt of Vitamin C.

Juice prep to finish: 10 minutes

Difficulty: Easy

Yield: (1) 8 oz. glass

Ingredients:
- 6 green leafy lettuce leaves, washed
- Generous handful of fresh spinach
- 1 handful alfalfa sprouts
- 2 oranges, peeled, sectioned
- Ice, optional

Instructions:
1. Bunch or rip up lettuce leaves and put through juicer
2. Process spinach and alfalfa sprouts through juicer
3. Process sectioned oranges through juicer
4. Pour into tall glass, over ice if desired, and stir with spoon to ensure juice is well blended.
5. Drink juice as soon as possible to benefit from full amount of nutrients.

Nutritional info:
- Calories: 118 -
- Total Fat: 2.3g-
- Total Carbohydrates: 23.8g-
- Dietary Fiber: 2.5g-
- Sugars: 15.2g-
- Protein: 3.3g-
- Sodium: 17mg

The Fruit Cleanse

A tasty way to a full body cleansing - This is a great change of pace from all of the vegetables you consume during a cleanse/detox program. Remember, however, that the reason we use mainly vegetables during cleanses is to keep the sugar content as minimal as possible – so while this juice provides a nice change, it should only be used sporadically – no more than once per week during your detox program.

Juice prep to finish: 10 minutes

Difficulty: Easy

Yield: (1) 8 oz. glass

Ingredients:
- 3 apples, washed and wedged (seeds are okay to juice for adults)
- 2 cups watermelon, cubes
- 1 kiwi, peeled
- 1 lime, peeled
- Ice, optional

Instructions:
1. Juice apples, cut into smaller chunks if wedges are too large for your juicer's feed tube.
2. Next juice watermelon, kiwi, and lime.
3. Once juiced, pour juice into tall glass, over ice if preferred.
4. Drink juice as soon as possible to benefit from full amount of nutrients.

Nutritional info:
- Calories: 158
- Total Fat: 3.2g
- Total Carbohydrates: 17.8g
- Dietary Fiber: 3g
- Sugars: 2.8g
- Protein: 1.3g
- Sodium: 4mg

The Green Lemonade Cleanser

A favorite of many detox juicers! This full body cleanse tastes amazing with fresh romaine, sweet apples, and lemon – and safe enough to enjoy daily!

Juice prep to finish: 15 minutes

Difficulty: Easy

Yield: (2) 8 oz. glass

Ingredients:
- One head romaine lettuce, washed
- 5 – 6 stalks of kale, rinsed
- 2 apples, washed and wedged, (I prefer Fuji for the sweetness, the sweeter the apples in this juice the better)
- 1 lemon, peeled (if organic, you can juice with peel intact)
- 1 – 2 tablespoons fresh gingerroot (optional, per preferred taste)
- Ice (optional)

Instructions:
1. Process romaine lettuce into juicer.
2. Process kale, apples, and lemon into juicer,
3. Add 1 to 2 tablespoons of gingerroot, more or less to taste (optional)
4. Once juiced, pour juice into tall glass, over ice if preferred.
5. Drink juice as soon as possible to benefit from full amount of nutrients, remaining juice may be stored in the fridge in an airtight, opaque container to protect from heat, light, and air exposure for 24 hours.

Nutritional info:
- Calories: 119
- Total Fat: 1.2g
- Total Carbohydrates: 4.8g
- Dietary Fiber: 0.7g
- Sugars: 3.8g
- Protein: 6.5g
- Sodium: 4.2mg

The Eye-Opener

This juice is great to drink if you are feeling weak or sluggish either during your detox program or just a midday energy crash at work. Great for everyone whether you are on a cleansing program or not! A real eye-opener and revitalizer, it will provide you with the pickup you need and get you moving again. This juice is stacked with so many wonderful nutrients, vitamins, and minerals.
Note*: Best to use a blender and juicer with this one.*

Juice prep to finish: 15-20 minutes

Difficulty: Intermediate

Yield: (1) 8 oz. glass

Ingredients:
- 2 apricots, peeled and pitted - OR - 4 dried apricots, soaked overnight
- 2 oranges, peeled and sectioned with pith intact
- 1 medium fennel bulb
- ½ red pepper, seeds removed
- ½ yellow pepper, seeds removed
- 1 tablespoon molasses

Instructions:
1. In juicer, process oranges with pith, fennel, red and yellow peppers.
2. Transfer juice to blender, add apricots and molasses (add ice if you want a blended drink)
3. Blend.
4. When finished pour juice into tall glass, over ice if preferred.
5. Drink juice as soon as possible to benefit from full amount of nutrients.

Nutritional info:
- Calories: 68
- Total Fat: 1.4g
- Total Carbohydrates: 7.4g
- Dietary Fiber: 1.8g
- Sugars: 4.8g
- Protein: .07g
- Sodium: 21.8mg

Juicing for Weight Loss

If you are considering beginning a juicing regimen for weight loss I encourage you to do one thing first. Close your eyes...take a deep breath in...then exhale. Now completely clear your mind of one very common misconception about juicing for weight loss.

Juicing in NO way should ever be considered or referred to as a 'fad diet'. It just doesn't match up with the criteria. Here are some important clues to help you find a REAL fad diet.

Fad diets are typically only followed for a short amount of time, anywhere from 1 day to 2 weeks. There are a few 30 day fad diets; however, prolonged use of these types of diets can be dangerous, causing adverse reactions, negative side effects, and major health concerns.

The dieter is usually promised a large amount of weight loss at an extremely fast and harmful rate. However, the moment the diet ends, the weight almost always comes back. Usually, you end up with even more fat than you began with.

Fad diets typically involve the consumption of toxic and unhealthy substances such as chemicals, gels, pills, lotions and creams, etc., which can cause more risks to your health than benefits.

Some of the popular fad or "yo-yo" diets that many have tried (and then dumped for juicing) include The Blood Type Diet, The Hollywood Diet, The Chocolate Diet, The Slim Spray Diet, The Popcorn Diet, The Sleeping Beauty Diet, etc. There was even a diet called "The Calories Don't Count Diet".

These are just a few of the thousands and thousands of fad diets – Those who have ever struggled with weight will be among the first to admit that they have probably tried practically every yo-yo, fly-by-night fad diet that has ever graced the pages of a magazine. Many of us are so desperate to lose weight that we could probably be talked into just about ANYTHING if there is a promise of "becoming skinny". Honestly, just throw the word "diet" behind a phrase, chances are you'd get some takers. How about the Battery Acid Diet or the Toxic Scum Diet?

There is not much difference between nuclear waste and a lot of these so-called-diets. If you really break down all these programs and substances the corporations are throwing out there, you'd be shocked.

Which is why juicing can blast these cheap corporation-made diet-wannabes to smithereens. After all, only you know what you put in your juice. You can change it if you want to. And it all tastes terrific!

Juicing for Weight Loss Guidelines and Tips

Juicing for weight loss is probably one of the easiest ways to lose weight and become healthier. There are not a ton of rules or requirements. Just make sure you're listening to your body – it will tell you if you are pushing yourself too hard. That being said, let's move on to ingredients.

Creating Juicing Recipes

Before we get down to business, let's look over your options. Some of the common fruits and veggies that aid in weight loss include:

Apple – Low glycemic load which helps regulate blood sugar which in turn leads to weight loss.
Carrot – Because of its sweetness carrots will help to kill cravings. They also support liver health, and boost digestion. They also carry high levels of beta-carotene which act as powerful antioxidants.
Citrus Fruits – Fruits such as grapefruits and lemons have long been praised for the powerful effects they have on fat burning, metabolism, and weight loss.
Cucumber – Perfect for weight loss juice recipes as they are super low in calories.
Celery – Because celery, like cucumber is low in calories and water dense, it makes a perfect veggie for weight loss juices – The greens are also packed with nutrients which help in maintaining a healthy weight.
Lettuce – Very popular in weight loss juices as dark-green lettuces contain high-alkaline levels and are very rich in minerals which is important in losing weight.
Cabbage – A powerful full body cleanser that is very important in weight loss.
Beetroot - Used in weight loss juicing to help sweeten certain high-alkaline produce juices that may taste sour or bitter.
Spinach – Frequently used in weight loss because of its many, many benefits. Mineral rich and alkalizing.
Tomato - Helps reduce acid levels, cleanses liver, and aids in healthy blood circulation – all important in weight loss.
Watercress - Used in weight loss due to powerful of an intestinal cleanser it is. It helps expel toxins and most important importantly it stimulates fat burning.

Make sure you're also choosing high-alkaline produce! Some of the fruits and vegetables that are good at alkalizing include:

- All veggies/veggie juices
- Lemons/Limes
- Avocado
- Grapefruit (if on prescription meds talk to your physician before substantial use)
- Watermelon
- Rhubarb
- Tomatoes
- Almonds
- Pumpkin, Sunflower, and Sesame Seeds

- Flaxseed
- Sprouts (including alfalfa, wheat, chickpea, mung, radish, and soy)
- Cumin Seeds
- Lentils
- Hummus
- Tahini
- Fats/Oils including Flax, Avocado, Hemp, Virgin Coconut, Palm, Borage, etc.

Mixing these in your juice recipes will guarantee some powerful weight loss aids.

Using Herbs in Weight Loss Juices

Herbs can also be very helpful in weight loss. I recommend the following.

Ginseng: Great herb in helping with performance. It will help provide you with the energy and endurance you need to be able to maintain strength and also exercise too. Exercise is just as important in weight loss as eating right is, so make sure you are doing everything you can to keep motivated and on track. This herb will definitely help in giving you that helpful encouraging push.

Yerbamate and Gurana: These are two other herbs in helping with energy. One of the common side effects of weight loss juicing in the first few days is fatigue. These herbs will provide you with powerful boosts of natural energy (no jitters, no crashes). That's equal to what you could get from a strong cup of coffee, but it's an even better natural energy that lasts without a yo-yo effect.

Cayenne: This helps in raising your metabolism to a level high enough where your body begins burning fat at a faster rate.

Garcinia Cambogia: Has long been a popular natural weight loss supplement.
Alfalfa: Helps suppress your appetite.

Juicing Recipes for Weight Loss

The Skinny Dipper

A great drink for weight loss juicers because it is very filling and it helps in calming cravings for sweets. This blended juice is nourishing, tasty, and low enough in calories that those juicing to lose weight can enjoy this drink daily. Enjoy!

Note: *This drink requires both a juicer and blender.*

Juice prep to finish: 15 minutes

Difficulty: Easy

Yield: (1) 8 oz. glass

Ingredients:
- 2 medium tomatoes, washed (sectioned if too large for juicers feeding tube)
- 1 celery sticks with greens, washed
- 1 handful parsley with stems
- 2 oz. live, very low-fat plain yogurt
- 2 oz. very low-fat cottage cheese

- 1 teaspoons brewer's yeast (available anytime at your local health food store or whole foods market)
- Worcestershire Sauce, to taste
- Ice, optional

Instructions:
1. Process tomatoes, celery, and parsley in juicer.
2. Transfer juice to blender. Add yogurt, cottage cheese, brewer's yeast, Worcestershire sauce, and ice (if desired). Blend well.
3. Pour into a tall glass. Drink immediately to benefit from all the nutrients.
4. Any remaining juice can be refrigerated for up 48 hours, in an airtight, opaque container as to not be exposed to light, heat, or air due to risk of oxidation and loss of nutrients.

Nutritional info:
- Calories: 182
- Total Fat: 2.4g- Total Carbohydrates: 28.4g
- Dietary Fiber: 9.4g
- Sugars: 10.4g
- Protein: 1.3g
- Sodium: 69mg

Watermelon Eruption

This is an excellent choice for weight loss juicers who are beginning to pick up their exercise momentum. The more you exercise – the more you sweat and juice will help replenish electrolytes, nutrients, and minerals lost through sweat. This juice is also wonderful for weight loss as it acts a mild diuretic and it will help boost your immune system as well. It is an all-around great choice for weight loss juicers.

Juice prep to finish: 5 minutes

Difficulty: Easy

Yield: (1) 8 oz. glass

Ingredients:
- 1 cooking apple, unpeeled, un-cored, and quartered.
- 1 cups watermelon chunks, peeled and deseeded
- 3oz. broccoli florets, washed and stems removed
- 1 handful watercress
- Ice, optional

Instructions:

1. Process cooking apple, watermelon chunks, broccoli florets, and watercress into juicer.
2. Pour juice into tall glass, over ice if desired. Drink immediately to benefit from all the nutrients.
3. Any remaining juice can be refrigerated for up 48 hours, in an airtight, opaque container as to not be exposed to light, heat, or air due to risk of oxidation and loss of nutrients.

Nutritional info:
- Calories: 113
- Total Fat: 4.9g
- Total Carbohydrates: 17.3g
- Dietary Fiber: 4.5g
- Sugars: 7.8g
- Protein: 2.7g
- Sodium: 4.1mg

Metabolic Gush

This is an amazing juice for getting your metabolism back on track. This juice is loaded with vitamins, minerals, and powerful immune system boosters. This drink will take care of your Vitamin A and Vitamin C daily requirements. This is an excellent source of Instant Energy to drink down right before a fierce cardio workout – this mango and melon juice will keep you and metabolism pumping.

Juice prep to finish: 5 minutes

Difficulty: Easy

Yield: (1) 8 oz. glass

Ingredients:
- 1 mango, peeled, stone removed
- ½ cantaloupe. Peeled and seeds removed

Instructions:

1. Process mango and cantaloupe through juicer.
2. Pour juice into glass, over ice if desired, and stir with spoon to make sure juice is well blended.
3. Drink immediately to benefit from all the nutrients.
4. Any remaining juice can be refrigerated for up 48 hours, in a airtight, opaque container as to not be exposed to light, heat, or air due to risk of oxidation and loss of nutrients.

Nutritional info:
- Calories: 116
- Total Fat: .44g
- Total Carbohydrates: 28g
- Dietary Fiber: 4.8g
- Sugars: 26.3g
- Protein: 3.4g
- Sodium: 37mg

Power Surge

This juice is a perfect partner to any weight loss juicing regimen. This juice is designed to provide the juicer with the power, energy, and stamina to make it through a vigorous workout. With the combination of your weight loss juicing regimen, exercise regimen, and the help of this juice - you will be dropping the pounds in no time!

Juice prep to finish: 5 minutes

Difficulty: Easy

Yield: (1) 8 oz. glass

Ingredients:
- 2 carrots - scrubbed, unpeeled, greens removed and ends trimmed
- 1 kiwi fruit, unpeeled
- 1 handful parsley with stems
- 1 handful of fresh spinach leaves

Instructions:

1. Process carrots, kiwi, parsley, and spinach through juicer.
2. Pour juice into glass, over ice if desired. Drink immediately to benefit from all the nutrients.
3. Any remaining juice can be refrigerated for up 48 hours, in an airtight, opaque container as to not be exposed to light, heat, or air due to risk of oxidation and loss of nutrients.

Nutritional info:
- Calories: 108
- Total Fat: 1.6g
- Total Carbohydrates: 39.8g
- Dietary Fiber: 8.1g
- Sugars: 19.3g
- Protein: 5.7g
- Sodium: 98.4mg

Thyroid Booster

Perfect juice for those with thyroid problems trying to lose weight, this juice will help to give your thyroid a bit of a boost if it's idle or help regulate a thyroid that's in hyper-drive!

Juice prep to finish: 5 minutes

Difficulty: Easy

Yield: (1) 8 oz. glass

Ingredients:
- 2 carrots – washed, greens removed, and ends trimmed
- ½ medium lemon, peeled
- 2-3 radishes with greens, washed

Instructions:
1. Cut to fit through your juicer than push carrots, lemon, and radishes through juicer.
2. Pour juice into glass, over ice if desired, and stir with spoon to make sure juice is well blended.
3. Drink immediately to benefit from all the nutrients.

Nutritional info:
- Calories: 72
- Total Fat: 1.2g
- Total Carbohydrates: 34.8g
- Dietary Fiber: 3.3g
- Sugars: 11.8g
- Protein: 19.3g
- Sodium: 89.1mg

Kelp Cooler

Kelp has been known in weight loss for speeding up metabolism, regulating slow/fast thyroid and in helping to melt fat off of hips. Kelp also offers many other benefits – such as helping with complexion, hair and nails, etc. This juice is nutrient-packed – it will leave you feeling great!

Juice prep to finish: 10 – 15 minutes

Difficulty: Easy

Yield: (2) 8 oz. glass

Ingredients:
- 2 large tomatoes - washed and sectioned
- 3 celery stalks – washed, greens removed, chopped
- ½ cucumber – peeled and chopped
- ½ green bell pepper – washed and chopped
- 2 romaine lettuce leaves – washed, bunched or torn
- 4 dandelion leaves, washed well (A handful of parsley can be used in place of dandelion if dandelion leaves are unavailable)
- 1 teaspoon dried crushed basil - OR - 2 to 3 fresh basil leaves
- 1 teaspoon oregano
- 1 to 2 teaspoons rosemary sprigs
- 2 teaspoons kelp (available year-round at any health food store or whole foods market)
- ¼ cup water (if needed to help dilute if drink is too thick)
- ice, optional

Instructions:

1. Process tomatoes, celery, cucumber, bell pepper in juicer.
2. Add romaine and dandelion leaves to juicer.
3. Finally, add basil, oregano, rosemary, and kelp. Ensure that juice is well blended, add water to juice to dilute if too thick,
4. Pour juice into glass, over ice if desired, and stir with spoon to make sure juice is well blended.
5. Drink immediately to benefit from all the nutrients.
6. Any remaining juice can be refrigerated for up 48 hours, in an airtight, opaque container as to not be exposed to light, heat, or air due to risk of oxidation and loss of nutrients.

Nutritional info:
- Calories: 161
- Total Fat: .94g
- Total Carbohydrates: 7.8g

- Dietary Fiber: 1.8g
- Sugars: 7.6g
- Protein: 2.9g
- Sodium: 38mg

Appetite-Be-Gone Juice

Probably the easiest juice to make – great for mornings where your alarm clock failed to announce morning's arrival. This is a weight-loss juice that is actually a very filling appetite suppressor. You will love the simplicity of this juice – but believe me – nothing is simple about the power packed behind this weight-reducing juice!

Note: *If on prescribed medications, please speak with primary physician before beginning this or any weight loss program. It includes frequent consumption of grapefruit which may cause adverse reactions when mixed with certain medications.*

Juice prep to finish: 5 minutes

Difficulty: Easy

Yield: (1) 8 oz. glass

Ingredients:
- 1 lemon, peeled
- 1 grapefruit

Instructions:
1. Process lemon and grapefruit through juicer.
2. Pour juice into glass, over ice if desired, and stir with spoon to make sure juice is well blended. Drink immediately to benefit from all the nutrients.
3. Any remaining juice can be refrigerated for up 48 hours, in a airtight, opaque container as to not be exposed to light, heat, or air due to risk of oxidation and loss of nutrients.

Nutritional info:
- Calories: 92
- Total Fat: 1.8g
- Total Carbohydrates: 22.4g
- Dietary Fiber: 0.16g
- Sugars: 2.8g
- Protein: 1.4
- Sodium: 2.5mg

Metabooster Juicer

This is an amazing juice for kicking your metabolism into high gear. This juice is loaded with vitamins, minerals, and a powerful B vitamin called pantothenic acid, which helps speed up metabolism and facilitate weight loss. Loaded with Vitamins A, B1 & B2, C and E as well which also help to speed up your metabolism.

Juice prep to finish: 5 minutes

Difficulty: Easy

Yield: (1) 8 oz. glass

Ingredients:
- 2 kale leaves, washed
- 3 to 4 broccoli florets, washed
- 1 generous handful of watercress, rinsed
- 1 medium cucumber, peeled and chopped
- 8 to 10 grapes (whichever color you prefer)

Instructions:
1. Process all ingredients through juicer.
2. Pour juice into glass, over ice if desired, and stir with spoon to make sure juice is well blended.
3. Drink immediately to benefit from all the nutrients.
4. Any remaining juice can be refrigerated for up 48 hours, in a airtight, opaque container as to not be exposed to light, heat, or air due to risk of oxidation and loss of nutrients.

Nutritional info:
- Calories: 59
- Total Fat: 1.4g
- Total Carbohydrates: 3.6g
- Dietary Fiber: 0.8g
- Sugars: 3.5g
- Protein: 0.9g
- Sodium: 13.8mg

Strawberry-Lime Spritz

Perfect juice to help kick soda cravings – this is a nutrient-rich soda alternative without the guilt, high calories, and sugar content that would result in a soda relapse. For those who drink soda more for the caffeine than the taste – the ginseng in this juice is a natural stimulant and energy source, leaving you feeling alert and energized without the jitters and caffeine crashes. Ginseng is also used in weight loss as a great source in speeding up your metabolism and increasing your body's ability to burn fat.

Juice prep to finish: 5 minutes

Difficulty: Easy

Yield: (1) 8 oz. (250ml) cup

Ingredients:
- 4 oz. fresh strawberries, hulled or frozen, thawed
- ½ lime, peeled and sectioned
- ½ cup (4 fl. oz.) soda water
- 1 teaspoon Ginseng powder (available anytime at any health food store)
- Ice, optional

Instructions:
1. In juicer, process strawberries. Then add the lime.
2. Add soda water. When well blended, add Ginseng powder.
3. Pour juice into glass, over ice if desired, and stir with spoon to make sure juice is well blended.
4. Drink immediately to benefit from all the nutrients.
5. Any remaining juice can be refrigerated for up 48 hours, in a airtight, opaque container as to not be exposed to light, heat, or air due to risk of oxidation and loss of nutrients.

Nutritional info:
- Calories: 117
- Total Fat: 1.4g
- Total Carbohydrates: 8g
- Dietary Fiber: 1.9g
- Sugars: 4g
- Protein: 3g
- Sodium: 8mg

Pineapple-Cucumber Number

Pineapple's weight loss benefits such as appetite suppression makes a perfect partner with the filling and low-calorie cucumber. Great juice to consume when trying to lose weight.

Juice prep to finish: 5 minutes

Difficulty: Easy

Yield: (1) 8 oz. (250ml) cup

Ingredients:
- 1/3 medium pineapple – peeled, cored, and chopped small enough to fit through juicer's feed tube.
- ½ small cucumber – peeled and chopped small enough to process through feed tube.
- 2 teaspoons psyllium husks (available anytime at any health food store
- ice, optional

Instructions:
1. In juicing machine, combine pineapple and cucumber and process.
2. Whisk in psyllium. Stir with spoon to make sure juice is well blended.
3. Pour juice into glass, over ice if desired. Drink immediately to benefit from all the nutrients.
4. Any remaining juice can be refrigerated for up 48 hours, in a airtight, opaque container as to not be exposed to light, heat, or air due to risk of oxidation and loss of nutrients.

Nutritional info:
- Calories: 175
- Total Fat: 1.5g
- Total Carbohydrates: 43.7g
- Dietary Fiber: 4.9g
- Sugars: 31.7g
- Protein: 5.1g
- Sodium: 7mg

Hunger Outnumbered

Hunger doesn't stand a chance against this weight loss juice brimful of hunger-reducing nutrients such as spirulina, which aids in appetite suppression. The weight loss benefits provided by this drink are plentiful. The celery works as a mild diuretic and helps in preventing fluid retention. The spinach contains chlorophyll, which is a fantastic internal cleanser, and the oh-so-helpful chili assists in speeding up the metabolic rate. Last, but not least the psyllium husks will help in producing a feeling of fullness. This juice is an all-in-one weight loss program in itself, don't miss out on all of the amazing benefits this drink provides – it's simple and it works!

Juice prep to finish: 5 – 10 minutes

Difficulty: Easy

Yield: (1) 8 oz. (250ml) cup

Ingredients:
- 1 small Serrano chili
- 2 oz. (60 grams) fresh spinach
- 1 celery stalk with leaves, chopped
- 1 apple – cored, deseeded, and sectioned
- ½ teaspoon spirulina (available year-round at any health food store)
- 1 teaspoons psyllium husks or slippery elm, if preferred (both available anytime at any health food store)
- ice, optional

Instructions:
1. In juicing machine, process chili, spinach, celery, and apple.
2. Whisk in the spirulina and psyllium husks (or slippery elm, if preferred. Stir with spoon to make sure juice is well blended.
3. Pour juice into glass, over ice if desired. Drink immediately to benefit from all the nutrients.
4. Any remaining juice can be refrigerated for up 48 hours, in an airtight, opaque container as to not be exposed to light, heat, or air due to risk of oxidation and l0oss of nutrients.

Nutritional info:
- Calories: 87
- Total Fat: 1.6g
- Total Carbohydrates: 17g
- Dietary Fiber: 2.4g
- Sugars: 11.8g
- Protein: 2.3g
- Sodium: 2.3mg

Banana Apple Juice

Perfect recipe for weight loss juicing as this juice will keep you feeling full for a long time, will kill any sugar cravings, will give you ample energy for working out, and so many other amazing benefits all while only coming in at around 179 calories per 8 oz. cup!

Note: *Both juicer and blender needed to prepare this juice.*

Juice prep to finish: 5 – 10 minutes

Difficulty: Easy

Yield: (1) 8 oz. (250ml) cup

Ingredients:
- 1 frozen banana, chopped (either freeze banana for 5-6 hours ahead of time or buy a bag of frozen bananas at the grocery store)
- 1½ - 2 apples (Jonagold or Fuji preferred, but any choice will do) washed, cored, and chopped to size to fit juicer's feed tube.
- ice, optional

Instructions:
1. In juicing machine, process apple
2. Transfer extracted apple juice to blender
3. Add frozen banana to blender.
4. Blend for 15-30 seconds or until thoroughly blended.
5. Add more ice, if preferred, to blender to make juice thicker.
6. Pour juice into glass, over ice if desired. Drink immediately to benefit from all the nutrients.
7. Any remaining juice can be refrigerated for up 48 hours, in an airtight, opaque container as to not be exposed to light, heat, or air due to risk of oxidation and loss of nutrients.

Nutritional info:
- Calories: 209
- Total Fat: 0.8g
- Total Carbohydrates: 54.6g
- Dietary Fiber: 3.4g
- Sugars: 35.8g
- Protein: 1.6g
- Sodium: 3mg

Just Dandy

Kick those sugar and sweets cravings to the curb with this juice recipe packed with fantastic benefits brought on by the satisfying taste of grapes and dandelion. This juice will easily become your weight-loss buddy as it keeps you reaching for your weight loss goals instead of reaching for the chocolate cake. It's easy to resist cravings with an option as sweet, enjoyable, and healthy as this juice.

Juice prep to finish: 5 – 10 minutes

Difficulty: Easy

Yield: (1) 8 oz. (250ml) cup

Ingredients:
1. 1 handful dandelion greens or if unavailable, 1 dandelion leaf tea bag.
2. ½ cup (2 fl oz.) boiling water (if using dandelion tea bag)
3. 1 cup red seedless grapes, washed and stems removed
4. ¼ teaspoon brewer's yeast (available year-round at any health food store)
5. ½ teaspoon wheat germ oil (available year-round at any health food store)

Instructions:
1. Begin by processing dandelion through juicer's feed tube -OR- if using a dandelion tea bag, place tea bag in a mug of boiling water, cover and steep for about 10 minutes then remove bag and let tea cool.
2. Next, process grapes through juicer.
3. Whisk in brewer's yeast and wheat germ oil - Stir with spoon to make sure juice is well blended.
4. Pour juice into glass, over ice if desired. Drink immediately to benefit from all the nutrients.
5. Any remaining juice can be refrigerated for up 48 hours, in an airtight, opaque container as to not be exposed to light, heat, or air due to risk of oxidation and loss of nutrients.

Nutritional info:
- Calories: 78
- Total Fat: 0.9g
- Total Carbohydrates: 21.6g
- Dietary Fiber: 1.8g
- Sugars: 17.2g
- Protein: 1.9g
- Sodium: 2.9mg

Jumping Jubilee

A fantastic drink to consume right before cardio workouts – it pumps you full of amazing vitamins and nutrients that will keep your body strong and moving throughout and long after your workout has finished. Great source of natural energy that will keep you alert, focused, and ready to go without having to go through jitters and crashes.

Juice prep to finish: 5 – 10 minutes

Difficulty: Easy

Yield: (2) 8 oz. (250ml) cups

Ingredients:
- ½ cup (8 fl oz./250 ml) fat-free milk or fortified soy milk, chilled
- ¼ cup (2 oz.) low-fat plain yogurt or plain greek yogurt, whichever preferred
- ½ cup fresh strawberries, sliced - OR – frozen strawberries, thawed
- 2 medium passion fruit (mango if preferred), halved and flesh scooped from peel
- 2 teaspoons wheat germ
- 2 teaspoons honey
- Ice, optional

Instructions:
1. Begin by processing strawberries through juicer.
2. Next, process passion fruit. Juice.
3. Mix together the yogurt and juice. Stir in wheat germ and honey, make sure drink is thoroughly blended. Blend in ice for a thicker-smoothie type drink.
4. Pour drink into glass, over ice if desired. Drink immediately to benefit from all the nutrients.
5. Any remaining juice can be refrigerated for up 48 hours, in an airtight, opaque container as to not be exposed to light, heat, or air due to risk of oxidation and loss of nutrients.

Nutritional info:
- Calories: 252
- Total Fat: 1.4g
- Total Carbohydrates: 41.8g
- Dietary Fiber: 2.8g
- Sugars: 36.8g
- Protein: 13.2g
- Sodium: 179mg

Grapewater Zing

A fantastic drink that helps kick your weight loss in to high gear. Grapefruit, watermelon, and flaxseed is a combination that works – on their own, each of these ingredients has been known to work wonders for those trying to lose weight, but by putting them together to work as one will allow you to shed those unwanted pounds in no time.

Note: *If on prescribed medications, please speak with primary physician before beginning this or any weight loss program which includes frequent consumption of grapefruit.*

Juice prep to finish: 5 minutes

Difficulty: Easy

Yield: (1) 8 oz. (250ml) cups

Ingredients:
- 1 pink grapefruit, peeled
- 2 cups watermelon, cut into chunks
- 1 tablespoon flaxseed oil
- Ice, optional

Instructions:
1. Begin by processing grapefruit and watermelon through juicer.
2. Pour juice into glass, over ice if desired. Add flaxseed oil and stir until well blended.
3. Drink immediately to benefit from all the nutrients. Any remaining juice can be refrigerated for up 48 hours, in an airtight, opaque container as to not be exposed to light, heat, or air due to risk of oxidation and loss of nutrients.

Nutritional info:
- Calories: 179
- Total Fat: 0.64g
- Total Carbohydrates: 38.8g
- Dietary Fiber: 1.2g
- Sugars: 22g
- Protein: 1.4g
- Sodium: 6.3mg

Salad Twisted

This juice is filled with the nutrients you need to keep you healthy and strong through any weight loss program. One glass will fill you up and keep you that way along with kick any cravings along the way.

Juice prep to finish: 5 – 10 minutes

Difficulty: Easy

Yield: (1) 8 oz. (250ml) cup

Ingredients:
- 2 medium tomatoes
- 1 stalk of celery, greens attached
- ½ cucumber, unpeeled
- 1 handful of fresh spinach
- 2 romaine lettuce leaves
- 2 carrots – washed, greens removed, ends trimmed
- 1 handful watercress
- 1 handful alfalfa sprouts
- 1 red apple – cored and wedged
- ¼ cup shaved coconut for sweetness (optional)

Instructions:
1. Rinse all ingredients thoroughly. Scrub the carrots.
2. Cut the tomatoes into quarters small enough to fit through your juicer's feed tube.
3. Roll the spinach and romaine into balls.
4. Cut the cucumber into sections
5. Cut the celery into sections.
6. First process the apple and romaine, using the apple to help push the romaine leaves through the feed tube.
7. Next, process the spinach and carrots, using the carrots to push the spinach through feed tube.
8. Next process cucumber celery, tomatoes, watercress, and alfalfa sprouts.
9. Pour juice into glass, over ice if desired. Garnish with shredded coconut for added sweetness (optional)
10. Drink immediately to benefit from all the nutrients. Any remaining juice can be refrigerated for up 48 hours, in an airtight, opaque container as to not be exposed to light, heat, or air due to risk of oxidation and loss of nutrients.

Nutritional info:
- Calories: 228

- Total Fat: 7.4g
- Total Carbohydrates: 38.9
- Dietary Fiber: 7.9g
- Sugars: 9.7g
- Protein: 2.7g
- Sodium: 38mg

Fat Blaster

A bit tart in taste, but great for killing salty and sour cravings - this juice works aggressively to speed up your metabolism and to increase the speed at which your body burns fat. The nutrients in this juice also aim at melting away the fat on hips, thighs, and buttocks. The weight loss benefits of this juice greatly outweigh the tart taste – you can also calm the taste by adding ingredients such as plain yogurt, soy milk, or coconut milk.

Juice prep to finish: 5 – 10 minutes

Difficulty: Easy

Yield: (1) 8 oz. (250ml) cup

Ingredients:
1. 1½-2 apples, Fuji preferred – cored and wedged (the sweeter the apple, the better)
2. ½ cup red seedless grapes
3. 1 teaspoon licorice root powder (available year-round at any health food store
4. ice, optional

Instructions:
1. In juicing machine, process apples
2. Process grapes.
3. Transfer extracted juice to glass, over ice, if desired. Stir in licorice powder. Blend Well. Drink immediately to benefit from all the nutrients.
4. Any remaining juice can be refrigerated for up 48 hours, in an airtight, opaque container as to not be exposed to light, heat, or air due to risk of oxidation and loss of nutrients.

Nutritional info:
- Calories: 168
- Total Fat: 0.12g
- Total Carbohydrates: 42g
- Dietary Fiber: 4.8g
- Sugars: 35.7g
- Protein: 0.9g
- Sodium: 4.6mg

Kiwitastic

This is a weight loss drink that can be used as a reward for meeting weekly weight loss goals. It's so delicious you will think you're cheating! This is a nutritious, low-cal drink, rich in so many wonderful vitamins and minerals that assist in helping you meet your weight loss goals. For an even sweeter treat, top drink with a tablespoon of whipped cream.

Note: *Best to use blender for this drink, as it is supposed to be a thicker, smoothie-type drinks.*

Juice prep to finish: 5 – 10 minutes

Difficulty: Easy

Yield: (1) 8 oz. (250ml) cup

Ingredients:
- 2 kiwi fruits, peeled and halved
- 1 banana, peeled and cut into chunks
- ½ cup orange juice
- ½ cup frozen mango chunks (or frozen fruit of your choice) – if using fresh fruit, be sure to add some ice.
- Whipped cream, to garnish (if desired)

Instructions:
1. In blender, combine kiwi, banana, and orange juice. Blend for 15 – 30 seconds
2. Add frozen mango and blend 15 – 30 seconds.
3. Add more ice, if desired, to make drink thicker.
4. Pour juice into tall glass, Drink immediately to benefit from all the nutrients.
5. Any remaining juice can be refrigerated for up 48 hours, in an airtight, opaque container as to not be exposed to light, heat, or air due to risk of oxidation and loss of nutrients.

Nutritional info:
- Calories: 262
- Total Fat: 1.3g
- Total Carbohydrates: 68.7g
- Dietary Fiber: 7.8g
- Sugars: 52g
- Protein: 3.7g
- Sodium: 5.9mg

Tropical Tiki Paradise

A tropical taste for your weight loss juicing regimen that will help you to resist sweet, sugary cravings while speeding up your metabolism and boosting your body's ability to burn fat and calories. A really delicious way to lose weight!

Note: *Use blender only for this one!*

Warning: *If you are on any prescription medications, please consult your primary physician before regular consumption of pineapple.*

Juice prep to finish: 5 – 10 minutes

Difficulty: Easy

Yield: (1) 8 oz. (250ml) cup

Ingredients:
- 1 mango, peeled and cut into chunks
- 1 orange, peeled and sectioned
- 1 cup pineapple, cut into chunks
- 1 cup watermelon, cut into chunks
- 1 slice of pawpaw (optional)
- 5 fresh strawberries, sliced – OR – 5 frozen strawberries, thawed
- Splash of either coconut juice, coconut milk, OR coconut water
- ice, optional

Instructions:
1. In blender, place mango, orange, pineapple, and a splash of coconut juice. Blend for 15 to 30 seconds.
2. Next, add watermelon, pawpaw (optional), and strawberries. Blend for another 15 to 30 seconds.
3. Add ice, to make smoothie thicker, if needed.
4. Pour smoothie in to tall glass and drink immediately to benefit from all the nutrients.
5. Any remaining juice can be refrigerated for up 48 hours, in an airtight, opaque container as to not be exposed to light, heat, or air due to risk of oxidation and loss of nutrients.

Nutritional info:
- Calories: 212
- Total Fat: 2.4g
- Total Carbohydrates: 51.8g
- Dietary Fiber: 4.8g
- Sugars: 32.8g
- Protein: 1.9g
- Sodium: 8.7mg

Apple Almond Dreams

A weight loss juice that fills you up and keeps you full – a perfect meal replacement juice for people on a liquid diet It keeps you on track with needed vitamins and nutrients, but it's also low calorie – you will begin to see the weight literally dissolve from your body. A weight loss juice recipe that tastes amazing and is safe to use on a daily basis!

Juice prep to finish: 5 – 10 minutes

Difficulty: Easy

Yield: (1) 8 oz. (250ml) cup

Ingredients:
- 4 large carrots
- 2 stalks of celery, leaves and greens attached
- ¼ cup fresh baby spinach
- 1 red apple – cored, seeded, left unpeeled, and cut into wedges
- 2 sprigs fresh parsley
- 2 tablespoons each lemon juice
- 2 tablespoons each lime juice
- 1 tablespoon vanilla protein powder
- ice, optional

Instructions:
1. In juicer, process carrots, celery, spinach, apple, and parsley.
2. Pour juice in to tall glass and add lemon juice, lime juice, and protein powder and stir with spoon until well blended. Drink immediately to benefit from all the nutrients.
3. Any remaining juice can be refrigerated for up 48 hours, in an airtight, opaque container as to not be exposed to light, heat, or air due to risk of oxidation and loss of nutrients.

Nutritional info:
- Calories: 132
- Total Fat: 3.4g
- Total Carbohydrates: 16.4g
- Dietary Fiber: 1.9g
- Sugars: 8.7g
- Protein: 1.4g
- Sodium: 1.8mg

Juicing for the Mind

Many juicers follow juicing regimens that help aid healthy brain function and assist with memory recall, Alzheimer's/dementias prevention, assist in strengthening concentration and focus, mental performance, as well as juicing for stress and anxiety relief.

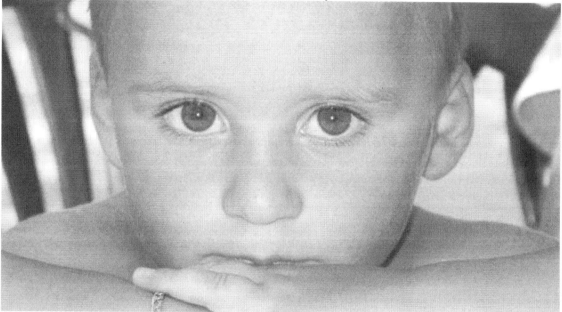

Juicing regimens that target brain function and mental performance are becoming increasingly popular. People are beginning to juice for their minds as much as they are juicing for their physical body. There are many ways that juicing can help you, and this perhaps is one of the most important things that juicing can do for you.

Having a healthy mind is more important than anything, you can have a perfect physical body but without a strong and healthy mind, it makes no difference. You need a strong mind to be able to function normally in life. The human brain is a miraculous and amazing work of art and should be respected and treated as such.

Just as we feed our bodies also should we feed our minds. Our brains function at a level almost beyond comprehension – they are never allowed rest, even when we sleep, our brains are still hard at work. They tell our lungs to breathe, our hearts to beat, our legs to walk, and our arms to carry.

Our brains are irreplaceable and we should not only acknowledge and appreciate this, but we should prove how thankful we are by providing them with all of the wonderful nutrients, vitamins, and minerals they crave so that they are able to function consistently at a high rate.

There are certain foods that we can feed our bodies that will target our minds to support peak mental performance. Foods containing high traces of Malic Acid are essentially "Superpower "foods for your mind. A few of these foods include:

Foods rich in Malic Acid:
- Limes
- Apples
- Peaches
- Rhubarb
- Nectarines
- Strawberries
- Cherries
- Prunes
- Fennel
- Tomatoes
- Grapes
- Cornsilk
- Pears
- Plums

Fats and Oils*: (argued to be the brain's most important nutrition source)*
- Flaxseed Oil
- Sesame Oil
- Olive Oil
- Hemp Seed Oil
- Evening Primrose Oil
- Fish Oils

Algae: *(used in preventing and treating Alzheimer's and dementias and improves memory function, increases concentration and alertness and aids in clearer communication)*
- Spirulina
- Blue-Green
- Chlorella
- Macro-Algae such as kelp, nori, dulse, and other seaweeds.

Foods high in Carbohydrates: *(Be careful with this one, especially if simultaneously juicing for weight loss – use in moderation. Carbs have been recognized to be a great source of energy for the brain – I'm sure you've heard carbs referred to as 'fuel for the brain', that is very true)*

I encourage those considering starting a juicing regimen for brain function to educate themselves on other nutrients, minerals, and vitamins which can be added to juice recipes to act as boosters in the juice. Research the different food sources containing Amino Acids such as bananas and sunflowers seeds. Vitamins E, C and B's, as well as essential fatty acids such as Flax Seed and Chia Seeds also offer many benefits in supporting brain health.

There are so many nutrients that can be added to juices that will do amazing things for your mind.

There are certain herbs that work wonders on healthy brain function and they can always be added to your juicing recipes with very little hassle. Just by taking an extra 30 seconds to throw some herbs into your juicing regimen, you will be providing your body and mind with immeasurable benefits. Some of the many herbs that are often used for healthy neurological function include:

- Ginseng – Targets pituitary and hypothalamus glands. Assists in treatment for insomnia and depression. Helps improve concentration and focus and increases blood circulation to the brain.
- Saint John's Wart – Reduces anxiety. Treats depression. It is used in prevention and treatment of several neurological disorders and it helps protect the brain from dangerous enzymes.
- Golden Root – Improves overall mental performance. Improves blood circulation to the brain. Improves concentration and attention span and is widely used in treating attention disorders such and A.D.D or A.D.H.D It also combats the harmful effects of stress.
- Garlic – Said to improve memory.
- Corn Silk – helps bind and remove aluminum from the brain which keeps the brain functioning properly.
- Ginko Biloba – Has been used for centuries to improve memory, cognitive thinking, and overall mental functioning. It also protects the brain against free radicals. Studies have shown that it is at least AS effective if not MORE effective as prescription Alzheimer's and Dementia medications as it helps in stabilizing, improving social and cognitive function, and helps reverse effects and helps stop the growth of certain memory disorders in people with memory disorders.

There are so many wonderful nutrients that are helpful to mental function. The list is enormous which makes it ideal for juicing regimens as there are so many choices in creating juices that benefit our minds.

The more you learn about these different foods, minerals, and herbs the more creative and precise you can be in creating a juicing regimen that is specific to your individual needs.

Juicing Recipes for the Mind

MINTal Tune-Up

Great juice providing your mind with a burst of nutrients that will improve mental functioning, focus and concentration, relieve stress, and more. There are herbs in this juice that will help rid your brain of free radicals and other harmful substances and replenishes your brain with a dose of really good nutrients. It's like oil change for your brain. This drink is also amazing for early morning meetings and workouts as it helps you stay alert and fills you to the brim with natural energy – it's like a really healthy double-shot mocha mint latte!

Note: *Best to use a blender only for this drink.*

Juice prep to finish: 10 - 15 minutes

Difficulty: Intermediate

Yield: (1) 8 oz. glass

Ingredients:
- 6 mint leaves, washed
- 5 brazil nuts, shelled
- 10 oz. soy milk

- 5 oz. live plain low-fat yogurt
- 5 tablespoons carob powder
- 2 tablespoons raw tahini
- 1 tablespoon lecithin granules
- 2 tablespoons wheat germ
- 1 tablespoon brewer's yeast
- 1mL Ginkgo Extract (1 dropperful)
- Ice, optional (either blended in blender for smoothie-type drink or "on the rocks")

Instructions:
1. Place Brazil nuts in blender first and blend until finely ground.
2. Add mint leaves, soy milk, yogurt, tahini, and lecithin granules. Blend for 15-30 seconds or until well blended.
3. Next add carob powder, wheat germ, brewer's yeast, and finally 1mL Ginkgo Extract. Blend another 15 to 30 seconds or until thoroughly blended. Blend ice now, if desired.
4. Pour juice into glass, over ice if desired. Drink immediately to benefit from all the nutrients.

Nutritional info:
- Calories: 119
- Total Fat: 2.4g
- Total Carbohydrates: 12.7
- Dietary Fiber: 1.9g
- Sugars: 17.8g
- Protein: 0.09g
- Sodium: 28mg

Watermelon Sweet Dreams

This juice offers many nutrients that help to calm and relax you. The fennel helps the body release endorphins which will aid in diminishing fear and anxiety as well as leaving you feeling at peace and euphoric. Many times the reason for Insomnia leads back to stress – it's nearly impossible to fall asleep and sleep peacefully when you are stressed out and full of worrisome thoughts. The nutrients packed in this juice will help in calming your mind and your body so that you are able to not only fall asleep, but stay asleep. Sweet dreams!

Note: Valerian is an herb which has sedative properties; it also calms the nerves and induces sleep – so it is important to only add this ingredient to your juice if you are preparing to go to sleep. You can skip this ingredient any time you need a stress reliever but sleep is not an option. Lettuce is also suggested to be sedating and carry calming effects as well; however, it can be added to this juice every time without concern.

Juice prep to finish: 10 minutes

Difficulty: Intermediate

Yield: (1) 8 oz. glass

Ingredients:
- 2 cups watermelon deseeded and cut into chunks.
- 3 to 4 iceberg lettuce leaves (Note: if juicing for weight loss – use Romaine Lettuce in place of Iceberg)
- ½ medium cucumber -peeled and chopped.
- 3 fennel stalks, leaves and flowers intact.
- 1 teaspoon of Valerian tea (can use chamomile if you prefer – either herb is available for purchase year-round at any health food store)
- ½ tablespoon brewer's yeast (available year-round at any health food store or whole foods market)
- Ice, optional

Instructions:
1. Cut watermelon and cucumber to fit juicer's feed tube. Bunch up lettuce and stick in feed tube, use the melon and cucumber to help push the lettuce through and juice.
2. Next add fennel stalks (keeping any leaves and flowers attached), valerian tea, and brewer's yeast and juice.
3. When juice is thoroughly blended, pour into tall glass, over ice, if desired. Drink immediately to benefit from all the nutrients.

Nutritional info:
- Calories: 162

- Total Fat: 2.4g
- Total Carbohydrates: 38.8g
- Dietary Fiber: 3.8g
- Sugars: 4g
- Protein: 1.3g
- Sodium: 14mg

Cucumber Slumber

Great juice for fighting insomnia and restless sleep – contains nutrients that will help to settle your mind and body. Rich in Vitamins C, calcium, iron, and beta-carotene and additional nutrients, this juice will help you in getting a good night's sleep. I encourage anyone suffering from insomnia or any stress-related sleep disorders to try this juice just once – because once is all it takes for this juice to aid in alleviating Insomnia.

Note: *Be advised – Parsley consumed in large doses can be toxic. A safe dose for therapeutic use should be limited to ½ cup per day to avoid any adverse effects. Pregnant women should abstain from the intake of parsley during pregnancy.*

Juice prep to finish: 10 - 15 minutes

Difficulty: Intermediate

Yield: (1) 8 oz. glass

Ingredients:
- 1 large cucumber, peeled and chopped
- 1 to 2 medium-large kale leaves, rinsed
- 1 handful parsley
- 1 celery stalk, washed leaving any stems and leaves attached
- ½ lemon, peeled
- 1-inch piece of gingerroot, scrubbed (peeled if aged)

Instructions:
1. Cut cucumber, celery, and lemon to fit juicer's feed tube.
2. Bunch up kale leaves.
3. Use cucumber to push kale leaves through feed tube and juice. Add celery and lemon.
4. Finally, push parsley through feed tube and juice.
5. Pour juice into glass, over ice if desired. Stir with spoon to ensure all ingredients are blended.
6. Drink immediately to benefit from all the nutrients.

Nutritional info:
- Calories: 78
- Total Fat: 0.5g
- Total Carbohydrates: 7.9g
- Dietary Fiber: 1.4g
- Sugars: 6.2g
- Protein: 1.3g:
- Sodium: 9mg

CocoBananaRama!

A light and fruity juice to wake you up and get you moving – designed to stimulate your mind and help you to remain alert and focused on the day ahead.

Note: Use blender for this one!

Juice prep to finish: 10 - 15 minutes

Difficulty: Intermediate

Yield: (1) 8 oz. glass

Ingredients:
- One banana
- One mango (seeded, stings and skin removed)
- 2 tablespoons fresh lemon
- ½ cup coconut milk
- 1 teaspoon wheat germ
- 1 cup crushed ice
- Shaved coconut, to garnish

Instructions:
1. In blender, blend banana and mango for 15 – 20 seconds.
2. Add lemon and wheat germ, blend 15 seconds.
3. Lastly, add ice to blender and blend an additional 15 – 30 seconds, or until well blended.
4. Pour juice into glass. Stir with spoon to ensure that all ingredients is very well blended.
5. Drink immediately to benefit from all the nutrients.

Nutritional info:
- Calories: 222
- Total Fat: 5.4g
- Total Carbohydrates: 42g
- Dietary Fiber: 8.8g
- Sugars: 17.9g
- Protein: 4.6g
- Sodium: 28.6mg

Attention Grabber Grape

Grabs your attention and helps keep you alert - ideal for Monday morning business meetings or for those days when you feel 'scattered'.

Juice prep to finish: 5 -10 minutes

Difficulty: Easy

Yield: (1) 8 oz. glass

Ingredients:
- 2 cups purple or black grapes
- 1 cup fresh, sliced strawberries – OR – 1 cup frozen strawberries, thawed
- 1 apple, cored and wedged
- 2 tablespoons ginseng powder (available anytime at any health food store.
- Pure water, to taste

Instructions:
1. Cut and process apple to fit juicer's feed tube.
2. Next, process grapes and strawberries through juicer.
3. Pour juice into glass. Add ginseng powder and stir with spoon to ensure that all ingredients are very well blended.
4. Add ice and pure water to juice, if desired.
5. Drink immediately to benefit from all the nutrients.

Nutritional info:
- Calories: 193
- Total Fat: 1.7g
- Total Carbohydrates: 52.4g
- Dietary Fiber: 5.9g
- Sugars: 52g
- Protein: 3.3g
- Sodium: 6.2mg

Blueberry Oblivion

A delicious juice that aids in keeping the memory as sharp as a tack– the Ginseng helps in fighting off certain enzymes that work at diminishing memory recall. The Ginkgo Biloba, in addition to helping keep your memory strong, also assists in improving concentration, focus, attention span, and learning ability.

Note: Use blender for this drink!

Juice prep to finish: 5 -10 minutes

Difficulty: Easy

Yield: (1) 8 oz. glass

Ingredients:
- 1 cup blueberries
- 1 cup cherries
- ½ cup red grapes
- ½ cup raspberries
- 1 teaspoon Ginkgo Biloba – OR – 1ml (1dropperful) of Ginkgo Extract (available anytime at any health food store) May alternatively use a ginkgo biloba tea bag, if necessary.
- 1-2 tablespoons of Ginseng Powder (available year reound at any health food store)

Instructions:
1. In blender, process blueberries, cherries, grapes, and raspberries. Blend 15-30 seconds.
2. Next, add ginkgo biloba and ginseng powder. Blend an additional 15-30 seconds or until thoroughly blended.
3. Pour juice into glass, over ice if desired. Stir with spoon to ensure that all ingredients is very well blended.
4. Drink immediately to benefit from all the nutrients.

Nutritional info:
- Calories: 132
- Total Fat: 1.5g
- Total Carbohydrates: 29.5g
- Dietary Fiber: 4g
- Sugars: 18.8g
- Protein: 4g
- Sodium: 16mg

Banana Mango Bliss

A great breakfast option that will help to stimulate your mind, promote healthy brain function, and get you feeling alert and focused on the day ahead –

Note: *Use blender for this recipe!*

Juice prep to finish: 5 -10 minutes

Difficulty: Easy

Yield: (1) 8 oz. glass

Ingredients:
- 1 banana - peeled and sliced
- 1 mango - seeds, strings, and peel removed
- 2 tablespoons fresh lemon
- 1 tablespoon wheat germ
- ½ cup crushed ice

Instructions:
1. Place banana and mango in blender. Blend 15-30 seconds.
2. Next, add lemon, wheat germ, and ice. Blend an additional 15-30 seconds.
3. Pour juice into glass. Stir with spoon to ensure that all ingredients is very well blended.
4. Drink immediately to benefit from all the nutrients.

Nutritional info:
- Calories: 185
- Total Fat: 1.2g
- Total Carbohydrates: 42.6g
- Dietary Fiber: 5.4g
- Sugars: 29g
- Protein: 2.5g
- Sodium: 2mg

Watermelon Hydration

This juice provides a fantastic way to fight fatigue, hydrate your mind and body, and helps you to remain alert and focused – A great drink to consume daily.

Juice prep to finish: 5 -10 minutes

Difficulty: Easy

Yield: (1) 8 oz. glass

Ingredients:
- ½ cup seedless watermelon (rind included)
- ½ cup cantaloupe (seeds removed but rind attached)
- ½ papaya (seeds, strings, and peel removed
- 1 teaspoon chlorophyll powder (promotes mind clarity – available at any health   food store year-round.
- 10 fresh mint leaves
- 1ce, if desired

Instructions:
1. Process watermelon, cantaloupe, and papaya through juicer.
2. Next, process mint leaves.
3. Pour juice into glass. Add chlorophyll powder and stir with spoon to ensure that all ingredients are very well blended. Add ice, if desired.
4. Drink immediately to benefit from all the nutrients.

Nutritional info:
- Calories: 134
- Total Fat: 1.4g
- Total Carbohydrates: 18.8g
- Dietary Fiber: 1.8g
- Sugars: 19.8g
- Protein: 5.3g
- Sodium: 42.8mg

Alert Apple Tart

A juice bursting with nutrients that will help improve focus, concentration, and overall mental functioning - A tart, but delicious drink that you'll want again and again!

Note: *Best to use blender for this recipe!*

Juice prep to finish: 5 -10 minutes

Difficulty: Easy

Yield: (1) 8 oz. glass

Ingredients:
- 1-2 cups pure water
- 3-4 tablespoons sunflower seeds
- 1 apple, cored and cut into wedges
- 1 tomato, cut into quarters
- 1 tablespoon spirulina (a super food available year-round at any health food store)
- 1 teaspoon flaxseed oil (available year-round at any health food store)
- Pinch of Stevia sweetener, to taste

Instructions:
1. Place water and sunflower seeds into blender. Blend 15-30 seconds or until smooth.
2. Next, add apple to blender piece by piece and blend an additional 15-30 seconds.
3. Add the remaining ingredients and just enough water to reach a thick-shake consistency.
4. Pour juice into glass. Stir with spoon to ensure that all ingredients is very well blended.
5. Drink immediately to benefit from all the nutrients.

Nutritional info:
- Calories: 108
- Total Fat: 0.7g
- Total Carbohydrates: 29.8g
- Dietary Fiber: 4.8g
- Sugars: 24.9g
- Protein: 1.5g
- Sodium: 14.8mg

Ginseng Super Booster

A great way to support brain health and mental functioning – the combination of nutrients will help to improve memory function and recall. It is also an excellent source of energy that will keep you going strong all day long, without the jitters and crashes.

Juice prep to finish: 5 -10 minutes

Difficulty: Easy

Yield: (1) 8 oz. glass

Ingredients:
- 1 apple – cored and cut into wedges.
- 1½ cups grapes, stems removed
- 1 cup strawberries, stems removed
- 1 teaspoon Ginkgo Biloba
- 1 teaspoon Ginseng powder
- ½ cup crushed ice

Instructions:
1. Process apple, grapes, and strawberries through juicer.
2. Pour extracted fruit juice into tall glass.
3. Add in ginkgo biloba and ginseng powders.
4. Stir with spoon to ensure that all ingredients is very well blended.
5. Drink immediately to benefit from all the nutrients.

Nutritional info:
- Calories: 124
- Total Fat: 0.9g
- Total Carbohydrates: 36.5g
- Dietary Fiber: 3.4g
- Sugars: 32.8g
- Protein: 0.9g
- Sodium: 4.7mg

Juicing for Beauty and Healthy Aging

Juicing regimens to help support healthy aging, maintain beauty and vitality have long been used and experimented with. Just as there are juice recipes available for practically every illness and ailment, so are there anti-aging and beauty juicing regimens. There are juices for wrinkles, acne, cellulite, bright eyes, healthy hair, skin, and nails, hair thinning and hair loss, varicose veins, age spots, a healthy smile, and pretty much anything else one could want when it comes to juicing for beauty and anti-aging.

My take on juicing for beauty is this – I support it 100%. If a woman (or man) opts to pick up a glass of juice instead of a scalpel or harmful chemicals and substances to help in firming their skin or to help combat hair loss, then I am all for it. Sure, juicing goes much deeper than "skin deep", but I think it's wonderful that people would choose to juice to maintain beauty as opposed to exposing themselves to harmful procedures and experiments. We all want to age gracefully and stay beautiful for as long as possible. Juicing has been proven, over the course of many studies and trials, to help us in doing just that.

As with any juicing regimen, it is important to learn about the benefits from different food sources, vitamins, and minerals. It is important to know what is available so that you know how to get the most out of your juicing program. Learn how to improve and enhance your inner health as well as your outer beauty, as it is nearly impossible to have one without the other.

Other Ways to Use Produce for Beauty

There are many ways to utilize fruits and vegetables for beauty regimens which people have been practicing for centuries. While consuming raw fruits and veggies in juice form has enormous beauty and anti-aging benefits, there are also other non-edible ways to use your produce in your beauty regimen. Chances are when juicing you might find yourself with scraps of left over fruits and veggies. Here are some fun ways to recycle the leftover produce in ways that can also be part of your beauty routines and practices. Of course there are hundreds of natural homemade beauty and anti-aging remedies, but here are a few to help you get the ball rolling.

Facial Cleanser and Lotion – To clear the pores and cleanse the skin, combine 1 teaspoon milk, 1 teaspoon cucumber, and ¼ teaspoon lime juice into a shallow dish. Mix until thoroughly blended then apply liberally to face and neck. Leave on for 15 minutes than rinse well with cool water.

Cucumber Refresher – Helps refresh and replenish greasy and dull skin. Grate and squeeze juice from 1 small cucumber into shallow dish. Mix in ¼ teaspoon rose water and ¼ teaspoon lime juice. Apply to face and neck. Rinse with cool water after 15 minutes.

Cabbage Mask - This facial mask will help reduce signs of aging and combat wrinkles. Moisturizes and heals dry skin, leaving behind a radient and glowing complexion. To begin, grate and extract juices from 2 cabbage leaves. Add ¼ teaspoon yeast to extracted juices and wait for yeast to dissolve. Next, stir in 1 teaspoon honey until mixture is completely blended. Apply generously to face and neck. Leave on for 10 - 20 minutes, and then rinse in cool water with cotton washcloth.

Tomato Juice Lotion – Shrink open and enlarged pores by combining 1 tablespoon tomato juice with few drops of lemon juice. Apply to skin, then rinse off after 10 minutes.

Watermelon Water Freshener – This is an amazing way to freshen skin. Extract juices from 1 cup of watermelon chunks. Apply to face and leave on for 10 minutes, rinsing off with cool water when done.

Grape Juice Brightener - Make skin smooth and bright by applying 1 tablespoon grape juice to face, leave on for at least 10 minutes, then rinse with cool water.

Coconut Water – Drill hole in raw coconut, apply juices to skin to lighten and brighten and soften. Cover entire body, if desired, before stepping into shower.

Papaya Scrub - Excellent for removing pimples and blemishes. Rub finely-ground raw papaya to face and leave on for 20 minutes before rinsing off.

There are many other homemade beauty and anti-aging remedies, these are just a few of some very popular ones. It is amazing what all raw fruit and vegetables can do in helping keeping one looking and feeling young and beautiful. I encourage you to work at creating your own individualized beauty and anti-aging juicing regimen so that you too can experience all of the fantastic benefits that raw fruits and veggies have to offer.

Juicing Recipes for Beauty and Healthy Aging

Waking Beauty

A juice to revitalize you first thing in the morning - this juice leaves your skin glowing, your eyes bright, and your entire being feeling alert and rejuvenated. This is a delicious juice to wake up to in the morning.

Juice prep to finish: 5 - 10 minutes

Difficulty: Easy

Yield: (1) 8 oz. glass

Ingredients:
- 2 carrots, washed and greens discarded
- 1 Gala apple, peeled and wedged
- ¼ cup coconut milk

- ¼ teaspoon fresh ginger root, grated
- Ice, optional

Instructions:
1. Process carrots and apple through juicer.
2. Pour juice into a tall glass, add coconut milk and stir. Top off with grated ginger root to garnish. Drink immediately to benefit from all the nutrients.
3. Any remaining juice can be refrigerated for up 48 hours, in an airtight, opaque container as to not be exposed to light, heat, or air due to risk of oxidation and loss of nutrients.

Nutritional info:
- Calories: 134
- Total Fat: 1.2g
- Total Carbohydrates: 32.8g
- Dietary Fiber: 5.8g
- Sugars: 16.4g
- Protein: 0.42g
- Sodium: 89mg

Youth Juice

This is a great juice that leaves you shimmering with youthful radiance, looking and feeling young and vivacious. It is packed with many vitamins and nutrients which supports vitality and provides the juicer with strong, clear, and beautiful skin that positively glows.

Note: *You can also use the aloe vera juice directly on your skin for pore-penetrating skin therapy.*

Juice prep to finish: 5 - 10 minutes

Difficulty: Easy

Yield: (1) 8 oz. glass

Ingredients:
- 4 carrots – washed and unpeeled, greens removed and ends trimmed.
- 2 oz. aloe vera juices – either extracted from plant or purchased ready-to-go. (aloe vera plants can be purchased at any nursery or garden center. aloe vera juice can be purchased year-round at any health food store or whole foods market)
- 1 tablespoon blue-green Algae Powder or juice powder of your choice (Can purchase year-round from any health food store)
- 2 tablespoons Wheat Grass Powder
- Ice, optional

Instructions:
1. Process carrots through juicer.
2. Transfer to blender. Add aloe vera juice, algae powder, and wheat grass powder. Blend for 15 – 30 seconds or until thoroughly blended.
3. Pour into a tall glass, over ice, if interested. Drink immediately to benefit from all the nutrients.
4. Any remaining juice can be refrigerated for up 48 hours, in an airtight, opaque container as to not be exposed to light, heat, or air due to risk of oxidation and loss of nutrients.

Nutritional info:
- Calories: 124
- Total Fat: 1.4g
- Total Carbohydrates: 34.8g
- Dietary Fiber: 8.3g
- Sugars: 18g
- Protein: 1.4g
- Sodium: 189mg

Strawberry and Coconut Whip

A delicious way to crystal clear skin that glows! Containing a fantastic mix of strawberries, coconut, pear, and oranges, this drink provides a great source of a variety of nutrients that will assist in keeping you looking and feeling young and beautiful. This drink is an ideal addition to your daily beauty regimen – for just pennies a day, this drink can offer you just as fabulous of results as the hundreds of dollars being spent on anti-aging creams, serums, and facials. A must-try – you will be overjoyed with the results.

Juice prep to finish: 5 - 10 minutes

Difficulty: Easy

Yield: (1) 8 oz. glass

Ingredients:
- 4 oz. (125 grams) fresh strawberries, hulled - OR – frozen strawberries, thawed
- ½ cup coconut milk
- ½ medium pear, chopped
- 1 orange, peeled and sectioned
- Shaved coconut, to garnish (optional)
- Ice, optional

Instructions:
1. Begin by first processing strawberries through your juicer's feed tube.
2. Next, process pear, then the orange slices.
3. Transfer the extracted fruit juice to a blender, add coconut milk and ice. Blend for 15-30 seconds or until thoroughly blended,
4. Pour into a tall glass and garnish with shaved coconut, if interested. Drink immediately to benefit from all the nutrients.
5. Any remaining juice can be refrigerated for up 48 hours, in an airtight, opaque container as to not be exposed to light, heat, or air due to risk of oxidation and loss of nutrients.

Nutritional info:
- Calories: 92
- Total Fat: 0.07g
- Total Carbohydrates: 38g
- Dietary Fiber: 2.4g
- Sugars: 17.5g
- Protein: 0.7g
- Sodium: 12mg

Grape Float

Protect your skin from acne, eczema, age spots, wrinkles, and other damaging forces with this delicious drink. Filled to the brim with beneficial nutrients that will help to protect your skin from harmful exposure, such as Vitamin C which assists in boosting collagen synthesis and in neutralizing free radicals, and B vitamins that help give your skin a healthy glow, fight aging, keep your skin feeling hydrated,

Note*: If on prescribed medications, please speak with primary physician before beginning this or any weight loss program which includes frequent consumption of grapefruit.*

Juice prep to finish: 5 - 10 minutes

Difficulty: Easy

Yield: (1) 8 oz. glass

Ingredients:
- 2 cups red grapes, stems removed
- ½ grapefruit, peeled and sectioned
- ½ cup plain yogurt
- 1 teaspoon spirulina (available year-round at any health food store
- Ice, optional

Instructions:
1. Begin by first processing the grapes and grapefruit through juicer's feed tube.
2. Transfer the extracted fruit juice to a blender, add yogurt, spirulina and ice. Blend for 15-30 seconds or until thoroughly blended,
3. Pour into a tall glass and garnish with shaved coconut, if interested. Drink immediately to benefit from all the nutrients.
4. Any remaining juice can be refrigerated for up 48 hours, in an airtight, opaque container as to not be exposed to light, heat, or air due to risk of oxidation and loss of nutrients.

Nutritional info:
- Calories: 152
- Total Fat: 1.8g
- Total Carbohydrates: 42g
- Dietary Fiber: 2.6g
- Sugars: 39g
- Protein: 2.3g
- Sodium: 2mg

Plumberry and Coconut Potion

Fight against those pesky varicose veins, cellulite, age spots, and wrinkles. This drink works just as well as some of the most sought after anti-aging creams and serums when consumed on a regular basis.

Juice prep to finish: 5 - 10 minutes

Difficulty: Easy

Yield: (1) 8 oz. glass

Ingredients:
- 1 plum, pitted and halved
- 1 cup blueberries
- ½ cup red grapes, stems removed
- ¼ cup cantaloupe, cubed
- ½ cup coconut milk
- Ice, optional

Instructions:
1. Process the plum, blueberries, grapes, and cantaloupe through juicer.
2. Transfer extracted juice to tall glass and stir in coconut milk - blend thoroughly. Pour over ice, if interested. Drink immediately to benefit from all the nutrients.
3. Any remaining juice can be refrigerated for up 48 hours, in an airtight, opaque container as to not be exposed to light, heat, or air due to risk of oxidation and loss of nutrients.

Nutritional info:
- Calories: 58
- Total Fat: 1.4g
- Total Carbohydrates: 8.8g
- Dietary Fiber: 0.8g
- Sugars: 7.9g
- Protein: 0.3g
- Sodium: 13.8mg

Cucumber Greens Hydrator and Cleanser

A charming combination of cucumber, celery, apple, and other tasty veggies that will benefit you in a numerous ways - this juice brings amazing moisturizing, hydrating, and cleansing properties to your skin that will leave it feeling renewed and refreshed.

Juice prep to finish: 5 - 10 minutes

Difficulty: Easy

Yield: (1) 8 oz. glass

Ingredients:
- 6 stalks celery, washed
- 1 cucumber, peeled and cut in small enough pieces to fit your juicer's feed tube
- 1 handful fresh spinach
- 1 apple – cored, deseeded, and sectioned.
- Ice, optional

Instructions:
1. Process the celery, cucumber, spinach, and apple through juicer's feed tube.
2. Pour into a tall glass, over ice, if desired. Drink immediately to benefit from all the nutrients.
3. Any remaining juice can be refrigerated for up 48 hours, in an airtight, opaque container as to not be exposed to light, heat, or air due to risk of oxidation and loss of nutrients.

Nutritional info:
- Calories: 112
- Total Fat: 0.8g
- Total Carbohydrates: 15.4g
- Dietary Fiber: 1.3g
- Sugars: 17.9g
- Protein: 0.3g
- Sodium: 4.6 mg

Sprouted Secrets

A juice which gives your hair bounce, shine, and amazing body – the sprouts in this juice are packed full of nutrients which gives your hair lift and keeps it looking and feeling beautiful. Drink this juice a couple times per week to reap all of the amazing benefits sprouts provide and to maintain strong, healthy, and beautiful tresses. This juice is also excellent for healthy nails.

Juice prep to finish: 5 - 10 minutes

Difficulty: Easy

Yield: (1) 8 oz. glass

Ingredients:
- 1 cucumber (organic works best)
- 1 small handful of clover sprouts
- 1 small handful of buckwheat sprouts
- 1 large handful of sunflower sprouts
- 1 large handful of alfalfa sprouts
- Ice, optional

Instructions:
1. Process cucumber through juicer's feed tube,
2. Then process each type of sprouts, one by one.
3. Pour into a tall glass, over ice if preferred, and stir until drink is thoroughly blended. Drink immediately to benefit from all the nutrients.
4. Any remaining juice can be refrigerated for up 48 hours, in an airtight, opaque container as to not be exposed to light, heat, or air due to risk of oxidation and loss of nutrients.

Nutritional info:
- Calories: 42
- Total Fat: 0.4g
- Total Carbohydrates: 3.1g
- Dietary Fiber: 0.8g
- Sugars: 1.1g
- Protein: 0g
- Sodium: 4mg

Anti-Aging Green Juice #1

An all-in-one anti-aging miracle juice, this concoction does amazing things to keep your body healthy and moving and fighting the aging process. One of the excellent benefits of green juice is its remarkable power to leave you with strong, healthy, and radiant skin. Green juice not only treats, but also prevents blemishes and breakouts. I know many brides who consume a lot of green juice during the weeks leading up to their wedding so that they can walk down the aisle with clear, sparkling, and beautifully confident skin. But who says you need to be a bride to enjoy the benefits of this fabulous juice?

Juice prep to finish: 5 - 10 minutes

Difficulty: Easy

Yield: (1) 8 oz. glass

Ingredients:

¼ of red cabbage
2-3 stalks celery, greens attached
4-5 leaves of kale
1 lemon, peeled (unless organic)
3 apples, (the sweeter the better, so go for Fuji or other sweet-tasting varieties)
Ice, optional

Instructions:
1. Begin by first processing the red cabbage and celery through juicer's feed tube.
2. Next, process kale, lemon, and apples.
3. If using gingerroot, process it next.
4. If using ginger powder – pour juice into a tall glass and ginger powder. Stir with spoon until thoroughly blended. Drink immediately to benefit from all the nutrients.
5. Any remaining juice can be refrigerated for up 48 hours, in an airtight, opaque container as to not be exposed to light, heat, or air due to risk of oxidation and loss of nutrients.

Nutritional info:
- Calories: 212
- Total Fat: 3.6g
- Total Carbohydrates: 68g
- Dietary Fiber: 4.7g
- Sugars: 38.5g
- Protein: 1.2 g
- Sodium: 12mg

Anti-Aging Green Juice #2

You can get the same benefits from this green juice as the one before – both taste wonderful and are equally rewarding, so be sure to try a glass of each.

Juice prep to finish: 5 - 10 minutes

Difficulty: Easy

Yield: (1) 8 oz. glass

Ingredients:
- ½ pear, cut into pieces small enough to fit through juicer's feed tube
- ½ green apple, cored and seeded – cut into wedges
- 1 handful baby spinach
- 1 handful parsley
- 2 stalks of celery, leaves attached
- ½ cucumber, unpeeled and cut into sections
- 1 slice papaya or fresh mango (optional)
- 1/3 avocado (optional)
- 1 teaspoon ginger powder – OR – 1-inch piece of gingerroot
- Ice, optional

Instructions:
1. Begin by first processing the pear, apples, celery, and cucumber through juicer's feed tube.
2. Next, process the spinach, parsley, and cucumber – using the cucumber to help push the spinach and parsley through feed tube.
3. Next, add papaya OR mango and avocado (optional)
4. If using gingerroot, process it next.
5. If using ginger powder – pour juice into a tall glass and ginger powder. Stir with spoon until thoroughly blended. Drink immediately to benefit from all the nutrients.
6. Any remaining juice can be refrigerated for up 48 hours, in an airtight, opaque container as to not be exposed to light, heat, or air due to risk of oxidation and loss of nutrients.

Nutritional info:
- Calories 232
- Total Fat: 9.4g
- Total Carbohydrates: 32.5g
- Dietary Fiber: 8.4g
- Sugars: 9.8g
- Protein: 4.2g
- Sodium: 53mg

The Purple Pear

This delectable juice is created by combining a variety of different vitamins and minerals which are said to benefit the mind and body in many wonderful ways. This particular juice is made with nutrients and antioxidants that will rid your body of free radicals that can speed the aging process; it also has properties that will provide energy, calming effects, and induce a feel-good euphoric feeling. This juice will also help fortify, nourish, and clarify skin, brighten eyes, thicken hair, and strengthen nails. It will also assist you in maintaining a beautiful smile. For inner wellness and outer beauty, this juice is certain to do the trick.

Juice prep to finish: 5 - 10 minutes

Difficulty: Easy

Yield: (1) 8 oz. glass

Ingredients:
- 1 cup blackberries
- 1 cup pineapple
- ½ cup blueberries
- ½ cup raspberries
- 1 pear
- 3 sprigs parsley
- Ice, optional

Instructions:
1. Begin by first processing the pear, blackberries, pineapple, blueberries, and raspberries through juicer's feed tube.
2. Next, process the parsley.
3. Pour juice into a tall glass, over ice, if desired. Stir with spoon until thoroughly blended. Drink immediately to benefit from all the nutrients.
4. Any remaining juice can be refrigerated for up 48 hours, in an airtight, opaque container as to not be exposed to light, heat, or air due to risk of oxidation and loss of nutrients.

Nutritional info:
- Calories: 148
- Total Fat: 1.9g
- Total Carbohydrates: 34.6g
- Dietary Fiber: 5.2g
- Sugars: 23.5g
- Protein: 9.7g
- Sodium: 27mg

Free Gift : Top 40 Smoothie Recipes

To pick up your free copy, please visit:

http://thejuicingsolution.com/smoothies

If you enjoyed and benefitted from Beginners Guide To Juicing book, I would really appreciate you spending a few minutes to leave a review.

Printed in Great Britain
by Amazon.co.uk, Ltd.,
Marston Gate.